Devotions for Deer Hunters

Devotions for Deer Hunters
Copyright © 2006 by Christian Deer Hunters Association®
Published by the Christian Deer Hunters Association®
Silver Lake, MN 55381

The Christian Deer Hunters Association® name and logo is a registered trademark and may not be reproduced in any manner whatsoever without the expressed written consent of the Executive Board of the Christian Deer Hunters Association®.

All rights reserved. No part of this publication may be reproduced, stored in a retrieval system, or transmitted, in any form or by any means, electronic, mechanical, photocopying, recording, or otherwise, without the prior written permission of the publisher. Scripture quotations, unless otherwise noted, taken from the HOLY BIBLE, NEW INTERNATIONAL VERSION. Copyright © 1973, 1978, 1984 by International Bible Society.

ISBN 0-9772875-0-5

Cover Photo: B.J. (Bambi Junior) taken by Dr. Tom C. Rakow at Paul Bunyan's Animal Land near Bemidji, MN.

Dedicated to the Lord of the Harvest.

Acknowledgments

Special gratitude must be expressed to all the authors who helped make this book possible. Most of the entries previously appeared in the first ten volumes of our smaller booklet *Devotions for Deer Hunters*. Not only were these individuals willing to freely share their personal experiences or expertise with the Christian Deer Hunters Association®, but they have also helped the association through their finances and volunteer work. Indeed, all of the past and present members of the Christian Deer Hunters Association® have either directly or indirectly played a role in what you are reading.

Of course, the various contributions of auction items made by businesses and friends of the association over the years have been greatly appreciated. The Lord has used these individuals or companies (whether they were directly aware of it or not) to help make it possible for this entirely volunteer ministry to continue. In fact, your purchase of *Devotions for Deer Hunters* will also help advance the outreach activity of the Christian Deer Hunters Association.

Profound thanks to Beth Rakow for her long labor in typing the various entries, formatting the pages, making corrections, etc. To Dr. Phillip and Donna Wahlbeck, as well as Tim Wortmann for the many corrections and suggestions. Sherie Stroklund played an important role in the earlier pocket-sized volumes of *Devotions for Deer Hunters*.

One may notice that a significant number of the entries in the early pages of the book were composed by this author. The reason for this has to do with the fact that in the first volumes we were short on contributions from other writers. As time went on, additional submissions helped add variety and also alleviated the need for me to submit multiple submissions for new volumes.

This is by no means a perfect book. As managing editor, one of the vital decisions I chose to make was to let each author tell their story in his or her own words. Of course, sometimes portions of stories were edited for sake of space or clarity. However, we have attempted to retain the intent and vocabulary of each contributor as much as possible. Therefore, some authors might be more easily understood than others. You also may discover significant grammatical or syntactical errors. For this I must take the blame. Nevertheless, I trust that you will not let this stand in the way of the truth being conveyed by the various authors. Although some entries were composed by highly skilled or professional writers, most flowed from the pen of simple hunters. We have experienced Jesus Christ—and merely want to convey what He has revealed to us onto others. I am reminded of how the Lord used some common folk during the days of the early church in powerful ways. Regarding some religious leaders in the first century we are told, "When they saw the courage of Peter and John and realized they were unschooled, ordinary men, they were astonished and they took note that these men had been with Jesus" (Acts 4:13). We trust that you will also realize that we have spent time with Jesus.

It is our hope that this book will prove to be a great spiritual blessing to you. Write us and let us know how God has used *Devotions for Deer Hunters* in your life.

Dr. Tom C. Rakow
Managing Editor

Table of Contents

The Lord Honors Those Who Honor Him	11
He Knows Everything	12
Barnyard Buck	13
Deer Senses	15
Some Hide History	17
Sign	19
Is Your Faith Camouflaged?	20
The Opportunity	22
Before He Hit the Ground	23
Ask and You Shall Receive	25
Orange, Camo, and the Rainbow	27
The Antlered Doe	29
A Reluctant Prayer	32
The North American Hunter (Part I)	35
The North American Hunter (Part II)	36
God Can Use Anything!	37
Float Hunt	38
The Great Divide	40
The Ancient Tradition of Hunting	42
God Gives Us the Desire of Our Heart	43
Buck in the Shadows	45
All Shaken Up!	47
Old Antlers Never Die . . .	49
A Psalm in Living Color	51
Are You the Provider?	52
He Never Changes	53
The Lie	54
Confessions of a Poacher	56
A Matter of Moments	58
Don't Blow It!	59
God Uses All Things for Good!	61
Never Satisfied	62
Let God Be Your Guide!	63
God Got My Attention	65

Faith: An Essential Ingredient	66
Powder and Pull	67
Don't Forget the Light	68
Sometimes Prayer Brings Pleasure	70
Buck Fever	72
The Bug	74
The Unexpected	76
The Moose Hunters	79
God Never Misses	81
God's Grandeur	83
Does God Care about Animals and Birds?	84
The Storm	86
Undeserved Blessings!	88
Where He Leads I Want to Follow	90
Elk Hunt	92
Clearing the Brush	94
Water Holes	95
Pieces and Parts	98
An Invisible Wound	100
Should I or Shouldn't I?	103
Little Things	105
Make Your Shot Count!	106
All Things Are Possible	108
Go into All the Woods	110
His Eye Is on	111
A Red Flag	112
Adjustments	114
Keep It Simple	115
Being Thankful	117
Are You Comfortable Where You Are?	118
It's Only Temporary!	119
The Wrestling Match	121
The Old Rifle	122
Covering Your Blind Side	123
The Right Trail	124
The Hand that Feeds You	125
The Perfect Stand	126

The Ultimate Guide	127
Lost	128
Practice and Pressure	129
Be Ready	130
God's Fan	132
Trees!	134
My First Deer	135
My Personal Guide	137
Innocent or Guilty?	139
The Universal Hunt	142
Fundamentals	143
My Choice, to Be an Example	145
No Coincidence?	147
God Smiled on Me Today	150
Once in a Lifetime Moose Hunt (Part I)	153
Once in a Lifetime Moose Hunt (Part II)	157
What's Your Favorite Color?	160
The Grand Finale	161
The Fragrance of the Season	164

THE LORD HONORS THOSE WHO HONOR HIM
Scripture Reading: Hebrews 10:23-25

It was September, 1991. I hadn't bowhunted for about ten years. However, my son Tom wanted to start bowhunting and asked if he could borrow my compound. As it turned out, the pull on my bow was too heavy for him. So, I purchased a new one for him to use. After getting him started and scouting together, I got the urge to take my old bow and hunt with him.

The Friday night before archery season opened, our church was having a guest speaker, and I volunteered to be an usher. I knew the service would go pretty late. I also knew it would be hard getting up early on Saturday morning to hunt.

Nevertheless, I did get up and ended up having a wonderful experience watching two large bucks, an eight-point and ten-point, sparring just out of bow range. Even though I wasn't able to try for a shot, I felt blessed just being able to observe these two magnificent deer!

On Sunday morning I attended services at church, and Sunday evening I again ushered. I didn't hunt that day at all. However, when I went out Monday evening, the Lord blessed me with a successful shot at a six-point buck!

Upon looking back at that season, I feel God blessed me with this particular deer and the chance to see the two bucks sparring because I was faithful and put God and my duties at church ahead of my desire to bowhunt.

Prayer: *Heavenly Father, help us to ". . .not give up meeting together, as some are in the habit of doing, but let us encourage one another and all the more as [we] see the Day approaching" (Hebrews 10:25). In Jesus' name. Amen.*

Lyle Emme, Minnesota

Devotions for Deer Hunters

HE KNOWS EVERYTHING!
Scripture Reading: Psalm 139:1-16

Three of us loaded up and headed to Wyoming for mule deer. Having dreams of big mulies, we were finally on our way.

Opening morning we all saw deer. Several were nice bucks, but no one filled their tag.

The second morning we split up and were hunting on our own when I spotted a "dandy buck." I glassed this deer about three-quarters of a mile away. By the time I got there, two bucks were laying on the hillside. I couldn't see which one was the larger buck.

After glassing for what seemed like hours, I still couldn't tell which one was the bigger. However, this small voice kept saying, "That buck is bigger than it looks." Well, I looked and I looked, but finally slipped off the ridge to get out of sight. When I looked to my left, I saw one of my friends on the ridge. I signaled to him to get ready, and I stood up so the buck could see me. When I stepped over the ridge, the buck also stood up. My friend shot, and the buck went down. When we finally got to the buck, was I sick! Why didn't I listen? The buck's rack was twenty-six-and-a-half inches wide and five by six. I was happy for my friend, but I was sure mad at myself. When will I learn to listen?

This hunt caused me to think about how many times I've failed to listen when the Lord was telling me to share Jesus with someone. How often have I done my own will instead of His?

Prayer: *Lord, help me to trust You and respond in obedience. May others see You behind my actions. In Jesus' name. Amen.*

Jeff Burch, Wisconsin

BARNYARD BUCK
Scripture Reading: 1 Kings 19:1-18

I parked my car next to a shed and proceeded up the hill between the new church building being erected and the weed-filled barnyard. When I returned two hours later, it seemed as if the buck waited for an opportune time before busting out of the dried weeds. Although he was less than fifty feet away, he caught me so off guard I almost dropped my rifle. When I did finally recover from my juggling act, the buck was moving so fast, and I was so shaken up, he had little to worry about. I did get off a few shots as he continued to shrink in my open sights, but to no avail.

The truth of the matter is, after opening day, a person's liable to find deer just about anywhere—next to buildings, in a small patch of grass, or even in a barnyard. The buck you're after is probably still out there, but not where you would expect to find him.

So, it often is with God. He is sometimes in things and at places we don't expect. In today's Scripture reading, we learn that Elijah saw a powerful wind, an earthquake, and a fire. However, God was not in these. Instead, God was in something far less magnificent. You see, Elijah had often observed God working in dramatic ways. Previously, he witnessed a boy being raised from the dead (1 Kings 17:22), fire fall from heaven (1 Kings 18:38), and a torrential downpour ending three-and-a-half years of drought (1 Kings 18:45).

We also tend to think that God should always use the big, flashy things to reveal His presence. We expect Him to speak to us like the great Oz spoke to Dorothy and her friends in *The Wizard of Oz*. But God isn't as predictable as a Hollywood movie script. He often uses a child, a circumstance, or even a familiar portion of Scripture. What really matters is not how God chooses to communicate, but that we respond in the right way when He does.

Devotions for Deer Hunters

Prayer: *Father, help me to be alert and to respond when You speak. May I see You in even the ordinary experiences of life. I ask this in Jesus' name. Amen.*

Dr. Tom Rakow, Minnesota

DEER SENSES
Scripture Reading: Galatians 6:1-10

If you are like me, you probably have been amazed at the anatomy of the whitetail deer. Deer are equipped with two large ears just like sonar dishes that can hone into the faintest of sounds. They also have those two big eyes that can record the slightest movement. But probably the most powerful piece of equipment deer have are their noses with that keen sense of smell. As a serious deer hunter, I have always tried to keep abreast of the use of deer hunting scents such as rut-time attractors and cover-masking scents. There are many types of deer hunting scents out on the market, and I think they all have one main objective in mind. Obviously, deer hunting scents are designed to influence the deer's sense of smell in one way or another in order to improve the hunter's chances of success. In theory, when the deer smells the hunting scent, a combination of responses such as an increased curiosity level, sexual attraction, hunger, or reduced fear affects the deer. What happens next is the deer comes in closer to your stand and gives you a better harvest opportunity. The bottom line is that the deer is fooled just like a fish when it bites into a worm that has a hook hidden inside. However, I have found that I need all the help I can get because God has given deer their very keen senses. Most of the time I end up just smiling at how clever they are as they bound away from me.

There is also a spiritual parallel here, and I think it is related to how easily we as Christians can be deceived by sin. 1 Peter 5:8 states, "Be self-controlled and alert. Your enemy the devil prowls around like a roaring lion looking for someone to devour." Satan is the master of deception, and he wants to deceive us by neutralizing our senses to sin. He wants to separate us from God. But praise God that we have a way of escape through our

Devotions for Deer Hunters

Lord Jesus Christ. 1 Peter 3:18 says, "For Christ died for sins once for all, the righteous for the unrighteous, to bring you to God. He was put to death in the body, but made alive by the Spirit."

Praise God for His Son the Lord Jesus Christ and ask Him to help you to "be not deceived."

Prayer: *God, I praise You for Your Son, the Lord Jesus Christ. Help me not to be deceived. I ask this in Jesus' name. Amen.*

William H. Bernhart, Pennsylvania

SOME HIDE HISTORY
Scripture Reading: Genesis 3:21-24

Fur linings and collars can be of benefit to the wearer in the extreme cold that winter puts on our outdoor activities. When it comes to providing warmth against our skin, real fur is hard to beat. As the deer hunting that we enjoy takes us against the chill of a northern wind, the choice of proper clothing is a necessity. Animal fur can certainly help take the bite out of Old Man Winter.

During WW II, millions of animal furs helped keep our nation's troops warm on land, air, and sea. Some of the worst conditions occurred above the clouds as fighter pilots and bomber crews fought to bring freedom to a world invaded by dictatorship and tyranny. Airmen flying between 20,000 and 30,000 feet not only had to fight a foreign military, but the natural elements sought to claim their lives as well. With chill factors of well below zero, these riders in the sky, who spent long hours sitting still, needed clothing that provided ultimate protection. The military chose lamb skins with the wool intact called mouton. The skins were turned inside out to allow the wool to insulate the wearer. Pants, jackets, gloves, hats, and even boots were fashioned out of these skins of lamb.

In the first book of the Bible, Genesis 3:21, we read, "The Lord God made garments of skin for Adam and his wife and clothed them." Today it's doubtful any of us will be pitted against the extreme conditions experienced by the airmen of WW II. Fur trim, hats, and gloves don't have to go through such tests to be beneficial to our recreational needs.

However, as lamb skins provided protection for those airmen of the past, so, too, today there is a Lamb who provided for the salvation of every man, woman, and child. That Lamb is the Son of God, Jesus Christ. Asking Jesus to be your Savior can provide an endless warmth in your heart as you make your way down the deer trails of

God's great outdoors. Today, by accepting Jesus Christ, a lamb without spot or blemish, you can know for sure that your name is written in the Lamb's Book of Life (Revelation 20:15).

Prayer: *Lord, thank You for every perfect provision. Help me to share Jesus Christ with others. I ask this in Jesus' name. Amen.*

Gerry Caillouet, Ohio

SIGN
Scripture Reading: Psalm 8

The most successful deer hunters that I know have learned the importance of looking for sign. The fact is, even an elusive whitetail buck can't help but leave evidence of his presence behind. There may be a long, heavy track, an oversize bed, or even a highly visible rub on a thigh-sized tree. But in any case, a buck always leaves his mark. It's true that we may never see the rack that peeled back the bark, the huge body that made the bed, or the hoof that left the track. But, then again, there's a chance that we will!

The Creator of the universe who made all things has also left His mark. In fact, the Apostle Paul pointed out that the signs of God's presence are so numerous that everyone knows something about Him. As a result, no one has a valid reason for not acknowledging His existence. Paul pointed out to the Christians in Rome, "For since the creation of the world God's invisible qualities—his eternal power and divine nature—have been clearly seen, being understood from what has been made, so that men are without excuse" (Romans 1:20). Yes, God has left the prints of His invisible fingers all over creation. All that He has made carries a label that identifies Him as the Maker.

Prayer: *Heavenly Father, thank You for Your many signatures, but thank You most of all for Your Son, Jesus Christ who said, "Anyone who has seen me has seen the Father" (John 14:9). Amen.*

Dr. Tom Rakow, Minnesota

IS YOUR FAITH CAMOUFLAGED?
Scripture Reading: 2 Timothy 1:3-12

As a Christian have you accepted the challenge of going one-on-one with a fellow hunter? A deer hunter has to go where the deer are. As a Christian deer hunter do you go where the deer hunters are?

For example, many bowhunters by nature are loners, conservative, shy, cautious, do-it-yourselfers. They enjoy the challenge of going one-on-one with a big, smart old buck. If you are a bow hunter, do you look for opportunities at archery shops, shoots, ranges, clubs, and your contact with land owners? It is possible to place our deer stand too far off from the trail they are frequenting.

We all know how important scouting is to a successful hunt. Are we looking for the tell-tale signs of other hunters? Has any hunter ever expressed to you that they are having health, marriage, family, work, or marriage problems? Are they looking for a friend?

Being scent-free is especially important for the bow hunter who needs to get close enough for a shot. Are you squeaky clean? Is your life above reproach? Do you obey game laws, respect nature, and land owner's rights? Are you a positive example of a Christian in every respect of the word?

There are times when it is important to use attractants. Are other hunters attracted to us? Or, does what we do speak so loudly they can't hear what we say? Some attractants can scare off old bucks. Is our religious affiliation more important than the Gospel of Jesus Christ?

Have you checked over your equipment? Are you prepared for the hunt? Have you packed a New Testament or Gospel tract? Have you memorized some key Bible verses? Do you have a tee-shirt or cap that expresses your faith? Are you available to be of help?

Every deer hunter would like to harvest a trophy

some day. However, each and every lost soul won for the Lord is a trophy of God's grace.

Do I do the right thing each time I go hunting? Absolutely not! But that doesn't prevent me from going back out. I make adjustments and try again. Ask the Lord for wisdom and the right words. Let's sow the good seed of God's word. Let's not camouflage our faith!

Prayer: *Heavenly Father, help me to not be ashamed of Jesus Christ. Amen.*

Lee Seeley, Minnesota

Devotions for Deer Hunters

THE OPPORTUNITY
Scripture Reading: Ephesians 5:8-20

I had been standing in this point of poplar trees since first light after dropping off my friend Danny two miles to the north to push through a large tamarack swamp. It was now about 10:30 in the morning. I was cold and bored. I wished Danny would come.

As I stood looking at the snow I had packed down standing there the last four hours, my rifle leaning against the tree next to me, I heard a muffled grunt. My whole being was totally awake as I rolled my eyes to the left. There stood a nice ten-point buck at seventy-five yards with steam rolling out of his nostrils. As I reached for my rifle and brought it to my shoulder, all my strength left me for a split second. The buck detected my movement and, with two bounds, was over a deadfall. I got off two quick shots and never cut a hair on him. I had lost the opportunity. I had let the hours of waiting and watching lull me to an off-guard attitude and steal all the preparation and time it took to put myself in a position to harvest that nice buck.

In our walk with the Lord, we can become bored and impatient and miss opportunities He brings to us to further His kingdom. Let's not be caught off-guard and miss the opportunity to help enter the harvest for the Lord. Jesus said, "'I tell you, open your eyes and look at the fields! They are ripe for harvest'" (John 4:35). And again, in Matthew 9:37, Jesus said, "'The harvest is plentiful but the workers are few.'" Are you serving the Lord? Don't miss out on what He has for you!

Prayer: *Heavenly Father, thank You for the great opportunities You put before us. Help me to always be alert. In Jesus' name. Amen.*

Les Stroklund, Minnesota

BEFORE HE HIT THE GROUND
Scripture Reading: Romans 5:6-11

All had been quiet around me as I routinely examined every nook and cranny around the openings where three patches of woods stood about 100 yards from each other. My vantage point in the "Lightening Stand" was in an excellent position to intercept any deer attempting to get from one wooded area to the next. Suddenly—very suddenly—I heard deer crashing through the icy marsh south of me.

I knelt down in my camouflaged platform stand, using the railing to steady my .243 rifle. One by one the deer broke into the open field about 150 yards from me. The big buck was accompanied by a mixture of six or seven does and fawns. He was in the middle of the group, and there was no mistaking that he was a buck. The sunlight made his antlers look like a halo around his large head. Typical of me, I missed the first running shot.

But, as I have noticed, it was typical for a buck to stop in his tracks, trying to pinpoint the direction from which the rifle fired. Only the buck stopped, the others leaped at full sprint for the coverage of the closest woods. My second shot hit him just two inches from the top of his skull and midway between each antler. I witnessed in my scope a deer going down so quickly and so hard that it seemed he was pushed down rather than falling down. Once I was able to examine where I hit him, I understood that he was brain dead before he hit the ground.

Like most hunters, I have relived the taking of a big buck in my head. During one of those times, it dawned on me that in my life if I had "hit the ground," in a coffin-wise manner of speaking I was already dead—"soul dead." I walked among the living, had years pass me by, just like all the others living around me; and in all honesty, I often felt that there might be a halo above my head because I did many good deeds and sinned perhaps only a few times a week.

Then a man who cared enough about me to share the gospel of Jesus Christ with me showed me Bible verses which proved I was already dead, and that I had better set my account right with God before I "hit the ground," then it would be too late. The Bible says that now is the accepted time to proclaim that Jesus' death on the cross and, in particular, His resurrection from the dead is the only way to enter the kingdom of heaven. "For all have sinned and fall short of the glory of God" (Romans 3:23).

Hunter, don't let another minute go by without turning to God and acknowledging that there is nothing you can do which is righteous enough to erase the sin in your life. Invite Christ into your life as your personal Savior. When your body someday perishes and is committed to the ground, your soul will continue on to its everlasting destination. Once there, it will reside forever. Pray now, today. Why would you risk another moment? You might not get a second chance like many of my bucks have!

Prayer: *Lord God, thank You for doing for us what we could never do for ourselves. Thank You for making Christ ". . . who had no sin to be sin for us so that in him we might become the righteousness of God" (2 Corinthians 5:2l). Help me to share this truth with others. I ask this in Jesus' name. Amen.*

Michael Herman, Wisconsin

ASK AND YOU SHALL RECEIVE
Scripture Reading: Matthew 7:7-12

The previous hunting season I suffered an unknown life-threatening illness. As a result my western elk bow hunt was cut short. Furthermore, this didn't allow for any whitetail bow hunting either. I was looking forward to some quality bow hunting and ended up receiving my first black bear harvest permit.

To share the experience, I planned to have a friend videotape the first few days of the hunt, then my dad would tape the balance of the trip. After not seeing any bear during my friend's part of the trip, my dad arrived ready to go. The following day we took our place in the tree stands to start our waiting.

My dad and I have shared some hunting experiences, but they have been few and far between. So, I asked God if He would please allow us to see some bear so my dad and I would have this, our first time seeing wild bear, together. I even mentioned in my prayer that it wasn't necessary that it would be a legal bear but just one we could watch would be great. Later that evening we heard some noises behind us. Yes, coming to the bait station were three cubs and a large sow. It was the most exciting and uplifting hunting experience I can remember.

On another occasion that same fall I was on a bow hunt for whitetail deer with my daughter. She had never been able to see a deer up close in all of our previous excursions. Yes, again the Lord answered this prayer with a doe and fawn within ten yards. Just the excitement of my daughter's voice after the hunt and to have shared that with her was a blessing and worth more than any record buck! The Lord blessed that year of bow hunting with many lasting memories—and even a nice eight-point buck.

Prayer: *Dear God, thank You for answering our specific* *prayers. Help us to remember that the trials of life can be overcome and our prayers answered because of Christ's death on the cross for our sins. In Jesus' name. Amen.*

Steve Truax, Wisconsin

ORANGE, CAMO, AND THE RAINBOW
Scripture Reading: Romans 1:18-25

My favorite season of the year is the fall because of the beautiful fall colors and, of course, the hunting seasons. October is a month of orange and camo. Like many of you, I will wear orange hunting clothes for the small game, bear, and deer seasons, and I will wear camouflage hunting clothes for the archery deer season. God also uses these colors as well as all the colors of the rainbow throughout His creation. What a blessing it is to see the beautiful fall colors of the leaves as they change from shades of green to red, yellow, and orange. God uses various forms of camouflage as well. From the white spots of the fawn to the various colors of the forest canopy, we can see His mighty power.

In the Bible the rainbow is mentioned a number of times. Two Scriptures are found in the Old Testament (Genesis 9:13-16 and Ezekiel 1:28) and two more are found in the New Testament (Revelation 4:3 and Revelation 10:1). Each time the rainbow is mentioned, it is at a time of great judgment on the earth as it is after the great flood of Noah's day. The rainbow also points to God's great mercy and grace during these times of judgment and symbolizes His promises to His children.

What can we learn from this? Well, next time you put on some orange or camo, praise God for His mighty handiwork as you peer into His creation. Even more importantly, praise Him for His glorious Son who was sacrificed on the cross of Calvary and is now seated at His right hand. Acts 4:12 says, "Salvation is found in no one else, for there is no other name under heaven given to men by which we must be saved."

Prayer: *Lord, thank You for the vast array of colors and patterns You have created. Help me to appreciate more and more Your wonderful works. Thank You most of all* *for sending Your Son to this planet in order that that we might receive eternal life. In Jesus' name. Amen.*

William H. Bernhart, Pennsylvania

THE ANTLERED DOE
Scripture Reading: 1 Samuel 16:1-13

Where I grew up, deer hunting was, and still is, an important part of the culture. Each year a person from the local newspaper would walk over to the police station where many deer were brought to be registered. This same individual would then take a picture of someone who brought in a nice buck and then include it in an article about that year's hunt.

In 1971, at the age of fourteen, a photo of me standing next to a deer that had one antler ended up on the paper's front page. At first glance, it would simply appear that some young fellow bagged a buck that had half a rack.

Nevertheless, things aren't always as they appear. The caption below the photo stated, "Tom Rakow, a young hunter, registered this antlered doe at the police station last week. One of the antlers had been broken off and the one remaining was still in velvet." Indeed, things aren't always as they appear.

Although the reporter who had come to the police station and taken the picture stated that one antler had been broken off, this was not completely true. Actually, the doe had only grown the one velvet-covered fork. In addition, by looking at the photo in the paper it would seem reasonable to assume that the person next to the pickup truck's endgate with his hand on the deer's neck was the one who had harvested this whitetail oddity.

However, again things are not always as they appear. While it was true that it was my tag on the deer's leg, my dad was really the one who had bagged this pseudo buck.

When you come to think of it, there are a lot of things in this world that aren't always as they appear. Take for example the person who outwardly looks like they have everything (money, fame, looks, etc.). More often than not, this same individual is inwardly empty and privately miserable.

Then there is the criminal caught red-handed, but who gets off the hook due to some minor legal technicality. From a strictly human viewpoint, it appears they have gotten away with it. But again, things aren't always as they appear.

According to the Bible, "There is nothing hidden that will not be disclosed, and nothing concealed that will not be known or brought out into the open" (Luke 8:17). As the Apostle Paul wrote the Christians in Galatia, "Do not be deceived: God cannot be mocked. A man reaps what he sows" (Galatians 6:7).

I am reminded of a thief I heard about on the east coast who burglarized a house. For all practical purposes, it appeared that it was a clean getaway. Except, that is, for one telling mistake. When he backed out of the driveway, he backed into a snowbank. He drove away, but left the imprint of his license in the snow. The license plate was traced down, and he was locked up. Yes, this crook learned the hard way that things aren't always as they appear!

The Bible makes it clear that not everyone who professes to know Christ truly does. Jesus not only warned of false prophets who would appear to be one thing, but were really another (see Matthew 7:15), He also stated, "Not everyone who says to me, 'Lord, Lord,' will enter the kingdom of heaven, but only he who does the will of my Father who is in heaven" (Matthew 7:21). In fact, Jesus went on to say, "Many will say to me on that day, 'Lord, Lord, did we not prophesy in your name, and in your name drive out demons and perform many miracles?' Then I will tell them plainly, 'I never knew you. Away from me, you evildoers!'" (Matthew 7:22-23). You see, the Lord sees things as they are, not merely as they appear.

The good news is that God knows if we belong to

Him. As Paul told a young preacher named Timothy, "'The Lord knows those who are his,' and, 'Everyone who confesses the name of the Lord must turn away from wickedness'" (2 Timothy 2:19).

All who know Christ have something wonderful to look forward to. John stated, "Dear friends, now we are children of God, and what we will be has not yet been made known. But we know that when he appears, we shall be like him, for we shall see him as he is" (1 John 3:2).

Prayer: *Lord, help me to see things from Your perspective. In Christ's name. Amen.*

Dr. Tom Rakow, Minnesota

A RELUCTANT PRAYER
Scripture Reading: Hebrews 11:1-6

Early in my Christian walk, there were some things that I could pray about and some that I couldn't. Some matters, in my mind, were worthy of God's time and attention and some I thought were probably too trivial for Him. I was wrong, and God let me know in the most unusual way.

During the third week of November, 1987, I was busy with my whitetail guiding operations in Alberta, Canada. I was guiding a gentleman named Clay from Bridgeport, Texas, on his third consecutive trip to Alberta in pursuit of that buck of a lifetime. Clay was a model hunter.

The trouble was that in three years in my eastern Alberta camp, at hunting's prime time, he had yet to pull the trigger on one of those big bucks that made Alberta famous. Other less prepared and less qualified hunters had taken great trophies, but Clay was just plain unlucky.

By mid-week Clay had still not seen a bragging buck and was beginning to wonder if this year would end empty for him, too. I remember lying in my bunk at night, saying my prayers, and wanting to ask God to help me put Clay on a good buck; but I just couldn't bring myself to ask. After all, God was very busy with heavy issues of the universe—plus He had souls to save. I figured it like this: God would look after souls, and I'd struggle along as best I could with deer hunters.

The next morning I was horrified to find that a thick layer of ice fog had blanketed eastern Alberta. Dutifully, Clay and I drove off in the predawn darkness toward our hunting area fifteen miles away. It was a quiet and very slow drive without much conversation. We both knew the ice fog wasn't what we needed.

I turned off the main dirt farm road and headed off across a pasture overlooking the Battle River valley. But as darkness gave way to dawn, blackness turned to gray, and visibility was about three feet.

Clay and I sat in silence, both contemplating the unfortunate turn of events. All the while, something inside me kept saying, "Pray and ask God for help." After about ten very quiet minutes, I put my binoculars to my eyes as if glassing the river valley. There, with my closed eyes stuck into the binoculars, I silently prayed, "God, I know this is not a high priority to you, but I need your help. Would you please enable me to show Clay a good buck? Amen."

A few more minutes passed and then Clay said cheerfully, "We might as well go back to camp and drink coffee—we're not going to see anything in this fog."

"I'm afraid you're right," I sighed as I turned the key in the ignition. I turned the truck around, and I drove slowly for about 300 yards to where the trail intersected at right angles with the main farm road. I was halfway through the turn when I looked ahead and was stunned by what I saw. In fact, Clay and I saw it at the same time. Directly ahead of us, through an obvious hole in the fog which looked like a large tunnel, there was a huge whitetail buck bedded down with a doe at his side. We gasped in unison. I was thrilled to the marrow because I knew I was seeing an answer to prayer. God did care about deer hunters after all! I could barely control my exuberance.

What happened next was comical. The strange hole penetrating the fog made judging distance difficult. We both guessed it wrong. We tried a sneak attack, but we were right on top of them before we knew it. They jumped to their feet and ran off before we could recover from our miscalculation. Not getting the buck was not nearly as painful as not seeing one at all. Since then, I have wondered if I should have asked God to help Clay shoot a trophy, rather than to let me show him one. In any case, God did exactly as I had asked in my reluctant prayer.

My prayer life has never been the same since that incident. God convinced me that there is nothing He wants me to keep from Him, and I am confident that there is no issue too trivial for Almighty God. I am reminded of the passage in James 4:2 (KJV): ". . .you have not because you ask not." Now I take God at His word. Hebrews 11:6 (NIV) says, "And without faith it is impossible to please God, because anyone who comes to him must believe that he exists and that he rewards those who earnestly seek him."

Prayer: *Thank You, Lord, for caring about the details of life. Amen.*

Russell Thornberry, Alabama

THE NORTH AMERICAN HUNTER: AN ENDANGERED SPECIES? (PART I)
Scripture Reading: Genesis 1:26-31

The extensive teaching of evolution has been partially responsible for a distorted distinction between humans and animals. Because of evolution, animals and humans alike are being viewed very differently from just decades ago.

Today in most science classes, this theory is being eloquently preached on a regular basis. Not only does evolution place humans and other creatures on a similar plateau, but evolution ultimately undermines the unique worth humans have been assigned in the biblical record. The Bible makes it clear that humans are distinct from the rest of creation because they are made in the "image of God" (Genesis 1:27).

Prayer: *Father, thank You for sharing Your creation with us. Help me to realize the unique value of all creation and to see hunters and non-hunters as having all been made in Your image. I ask this in the name of Jesus. Amen.*

Dr. Tom Rakow, Minnesota

Devotions for Deer Hunters

THE NORTH AMERICAN HUNTER: AN ENDANGERED SPECIES? (PART II)
Scripture Reading: Revelation 20:11-15

Why are many people currently opposed to hunting? The answers to such a question would probably be too numerous to tabulate. But a primary reason for the anti-hunter attitude that exists today can be traced to the increasing influence of Eastern thought on our society.

Religions such as Buddhism and Hinduism have greatly influenced our thinking. Furthermore, some movie stars have helped make the concept of coming back to life in different forms very popular. This idea, which is known as "reincarnation," is presently being propagated through the New Age movement. Let's face it, even taking the life of a rat is difficult if there remains the remote possibility it was a relative of which you were previously fond.

But the Judeo-Christian principles upon which this country was primarily founded do not teach reincarnation. In fact, they teach just the opposite. God's Word makes it clear we have one life. In the New Testament book of Hebrews the Bible tells us, "Man is destined to die once, and after that to face judgment" (Hebrews 9:27).

Prayer: *Heavenly Father, thank You that we can "know you, the only true God, and Jesus Christ, whom you have sent" (John 17:3). Help me to live this one life for Your glory. In Jesus' name. Amen.*

Dr. Tom Rakow, Minnesota

GOD CAN USE ANYTHING!
Scripture Reading: Ephesians 6:1-4

My son Rob, who is in his twenties, shares an apartment with two other guys. When one of his roommates' dad died, it reminded Rob that I won't always be around. It caused him to rethink our relationship. As a result, he called on the phone somewhat heartbroken. He didn't believe he was spending enough time with me. He practically begged me to start shooting archery and hunting with him again.

The fact is, those father-son hunts from years past had made a lasting impression on us both. They were special times we will always remember. Now, we get together at least once a week to shoot archery. We're also looking forward to the next bow season when we will make some more memories.

Isn't God awesome! Not only can He use creation and hunting as a vehicle for building lasting memories, but He can even use the death of one dad as a means to strengthen the relationship between another father and son.

How about you? Are you building lasting memories and relationships with your loved ones? If so, thank the Lord. If you aren't, why not start now before it's too late?

Prayer: *Lord God, thank You for the opportunity to build relationships with other hunters. May my life encourage those I meet to want a closer relationship with You. I ask this in Jesus' name. Amen.*

John Hartelt, Colorado

Devotions for Deer Hunters

FLOAT HUNT
Scripture Reading: Mark 10:17-31

  This is a story of a deer hunt which took place a few years ago in Sauk County, Wisconsin. During the November hunting season my son Tom suggested that we make a float hunt on a stream called Honey Creek. It seemed simple to sit in a boat and shoot a buck. So, with a ten-foot flat bottomed aluminum boat, we prepared for the hunt.
  A little after noon that day, we took one vehicle and parked it next to a bridge for our return. With the other, we took the boat to the starting point about three miles upstream. We then loaded our guns and began our journey. However, about seventy-five feet downstream around the first bend there was a tree blocking our way—so we portaged past it. After returning to the water and continuing on, we encountered the same situation at about every turn. Not only that, but the bank of the stream was so high it was impossible to see anything! Eventually, we grew tired of portaging and decided to switch strategies. So, instead of dragging the boat in and out of the water, we tried pulling our way over partially submerged logs and through downed trees. What then transpired resembled something similar to an old Laurel and Hardy movie (I guess you had to be there!). I, for one, was hoping that some fellow hunters who were on a nearby hill observing this ordeal wouldn't find out who we were.
  At the end of shooting hours, we still had half way to go. So, we took the boat out of the water and proceeded to pull it through a woods and across a couple of snow-covered corn fields to a nearby road. Leaving the boat behind, we then walked to the car. We still laugh whenever we talk about taking another float hunt; but, the fact is, we've all gotten ourselves into situations without realizing just what exactly is involved. Nevertheless, Jesus

Christ has never misled any person as to what it takes to be one of His disciples. He made it clear that to follow Him costs everything. In Luke 14:33 Jesus said, "... any of you who does not give up everything he has cannot be my disciple." And again, "... if anyone would come after me, he must deny himself and take up his cross daily and follow me. For whoever wants to save his life will lose it, but whoever loses his life for me will save it" (Luke 9:23-24). Yes, following Christ is costly, but it's ultimately worth it!

Prayer: *Lord, may I be willing to confess You openly before others. Help me to remember the great price You paid at the cross. I ask this in Jesus' name. Amen.*

Bob Rakow, Arizona

THE GREAT DIVIDE
Scripture Reading: Ephesians 5:25-32

In recent years, there has been a growing chasm between some hunters and nonhunters. This division is not physical, but rather philosophical or theological in nature. And, whether we want to admit it or not, this gap doesn't seem to be narrowing. Furthermore, some of the inappropriate arguments that individuals from both sides have used to support their cause have clouded the real issues.

Take, for example, the positive financial factors that some draw on to defend hunting. Even though economic matters may be important, this type of reasoning never addresses the moral issue about which many nonhunters are asking. We also need to remember that just because an activity may prove to be financially beneficial to a few or even to many does not necessarily justify that particular activity (see 1 Timothy 6:10). Certainly there were some in this country who, in a past century, profited from human slavery. However, this never made slavery right.

With the same token, others have tried to take truths from the Bible in order to prove that hunting is wrong. The command, "Thou shalt not kill," (Exodus 20:13, KJV) has been used by some to say that God clearly condemns the taking of any creature's life. Nevertheless, to do so one must seriously distort the intended meaning of this Scripture and also remove the passage from its original context.

First of all, the Hebrew term which is translated "kill" by the King James Version addresses the taking of another person's life or what we commonly call "murder." The context of this particular Bible verse also makes this clear. And if Exodus 20:13 was intended for animals, why did God direct the Israelites to sacrifice sheep, goats, and cattle (Exodus 20:24), to stone a bull that gores someone to death (Exodus 21:28), and use certain types of skins in constructing the tabernacle (Exodus 26:14)?

On the contrary, the Bible reveals that we have a responsibility before God to speak what is right. This even applies to issues that pertain to hunting.

Prayer: *Heavenly Father, help me to see things from Your perspective. May I recognize truth by what Your word says. I ask this in Jesus' name. Amen.*

Dr. Tom Rakow, Minnesota

THE ANCIENT TRADITION OF HUNTING
Scripture Reading: Genesis 9:1-7

How long has hunting been around? It obviously predates compounds, fiberglass recurves, and aluminum arrows. We all realize that hunting existed long before the invention of double odd buck and black powder rifles. Hunting even predates the U.S. Constitution, the pilgrims, and Native Americans who were here long before the Mayflower arrived.

The fact is, to learn about the early history of hunting a person needs to examine God's word, the Bible. According to the Scriptures, more than four thousand years ago a man named Nimrod was the first to become famous for his activities in the field. Sometime after the flood in Noah's day (Genesis 6-9) and before the confusion of language at Babel (Genesis 11:1-9), Nimrod appeared on the stage of human history. The Bible says concerning him, "He was a mighty hunter before the Lord; that is why it is said, 'Like Nimrod, a mighty hunter before the Lord'" (Genesis 10:9).

Nevertheless, to arrive at the very fountain head of hunting, we must ultimately turn to God. It was He who told Noah, "Everything that lives and moves will be food for you. Just as I gave you the green plants, I now give you everything" (Genesis 9:3). Later, in Leviticus 17:13-14, the Lord gave the Israelites some specific hunting regulations.

Prayer: *Lord God, may I obey game regulations in such a way that my life reflects a relationship with You. I ask this in Jesus' name. Amen.*

Dr. Tom Rakow, Minnesota

GOD GIVES US THE DESIRE OF OUR HEART
Scripture Reading: Psalm 37:1-7

My first Wisconsin hunt back in 1985 was one with little planning. The day before the opener, I was having lunch with a Wisconsin native who had just moved to Minnesota. He was getting ready to leave for opening weekend. I started asking him questions about Wisconsin deer hunting, such as license cost, availability of land, etc. I also was curious as to the chances of an out-of-state hunter getting a buck. I liked what I heard so I called my friend Doug and asked him if he would like to join me for a hunt. After some negotiating with our wives, we were off to Superior, Wisconsin. However, we needed to get our licenses by 12:00 midnight in order to hunt the next morning. We tried numerous places, but were unable to come up with a license until 11:55 p.m.

Later, while at a restaurant, I jokingly asked a waitress if she knew of any good hunting ground. She mentioned a place near Bruel. So, the next morning with much optimism and fresh snow, we headed out to the woods she told us about. We weren't quite sure exactly where we should go so I told Doug, "I think we should pray and ask the Lord where we should hunt." So we did. I prayed, "Lord, we don't know where we should go, and we need you to guide us." Five minutes later, two eight-point bucks ran across the road in front of us. I think we received our answer—thank you, Lord!!!!

Three hours later, I was sitting in the woods just thanking and praising God for such a great day. Suddenly, a beautiful ten-point buck walked out from behind a spruce tree into my shooting lane. He stopped and looked in the opposite direction. I smiled as I raised my 270 and hit the mark. I again thanked the Lord. God truly does give one the desires of one's heart!

The next morning as we were heading back out to our stands, I said to Doug, "Let's ask the Lord to bless us with a buck this morning so we can get home early and spend the rest of the day with our families."

Doug said, "You pray, and I'll agree with you."

So I prayed, "Lord, we would like to get home early today to spend some time with our families, so please help us get that other deer we need to fill our tags." One hour later Doug had his buck, and we were in Minnesota by 8:30 a.m. and back home by 3:00 p.m.

The Lord cares about every area of your life including your family, your work, as well as your hunting and fishing. God is for you—He wants to help you in all these areas. Just as a loving father cares for his children, He wants only the best for us. Let God be your God, ask Him for help. Invite Him into your life, and He will supply all your needs through His riches and glory in Christ Jesus. The Bible promises in Psalm 37:4, "Delight yourself in the Lord and He will give you the desires of your heart."

Prayer: *Lord, thank You for blessing us with the opportunity to deer hunt. Thank You for balance, grace, and peace. In Jesus' name. Amen.*

Louis King, Minnesota

BUCK IN THE SHADOWS
Scripture Reading: Luke 16:19-31

He was grinding acorns between his teeth as he grazed his way within fifteen yards of my tree stand. I strained to see a shape. It was several minutes into legal shooting hours. However, the overcast sky and heavy foliage from the grove of oaks I was situated in shut out what little daylight there was.

Then as I hoped, this unseen chewing, shadowy form moved even closer. Minutes passed. First, a hunk of the buck's polished rack became visible, then his outline. He moved within feet of the large limb on which I was perched. I partially pulled on the string of my recurve—and then waited. I thought, "Why not reduce the risk of a miss altogether? After all, within a matter of moments it'll be a sure thing." But then, suddenly, without warning, he turned, trotted into the tangled undergrowth, and was gone!

I hunted that buck hard for weeks. Every time I saw the heavy, long tracks he left behind, I was painfully reminded of having blown it. I had waited too long. In an attempt to reduce all risk, I had actually created risk. Indeed, I still regret having passed up that shot.

Even so, according to the Bible, some will pass up something far greater. Unfortunately, many will spend all of eternity reminded of the fact that they blew their biggest opportunity of all. Namely, their chance to gain eternal life. They may remember a sermon they heard, the witness of a friend, or even an entry in this devotional book. In any case, the Bible states that many will wait too long before they respond to the Good News of Jesus Christ. As a result, they will spend eternity in the torments of hell.

On one occasion, Jesus Christ was asked, "Lord, are only a few people going to be saved?" (Luke 13:23b) He responded, "Make every effort to enter through the narrow door, because many, I tell you, will try to enter and will not be able to. Once the owner of the house gets up and closes the door, you will stand outside knocking and pleading, 'Sir, open the door for us.' But he will answer, 'I don't know you or where you come from'" (Luke 13:24-25). Yes, many will wait too long. Those who wait until tomorrow put themselves at great risk. For as the Bible says, "now is the time of God's favor, now is the day of salvation" (2 Corinthians 6:2b). Tomorrow may be too late!

Prayer: *Heavenly Father, thank You that no one needs to go to hell because You paid the price for our sin on the cross. Use me to win others to You. In Jesus Christ's name I pray. Amen.*

Dr. Tom Rakow, Minnesota

ALL SHAKEN UP!
Scripture Reading: 2 Thessalonians 1:1-10

The buck came busting out of a patch of brush and headed straight toward my tree stand. Within seconds he had crossed a field and was ready to jump a fence less than five feet from the base of my tree. At first glimpse of this wide-racked whitetail, my iron sights were drawn to his chest. However, I opted for the easy broadside shot he was bound to present. He approached the sagging section of barbed wire. Then, just as I started to squeeze off that one sure shot—CLUNK! The side of my rifle hit a limb. I panicked and fired a poor shot anyway—it clearly missed. He bounded over the fence as I awkwardly managed to get my rifle to the other side of the large limb. However, the lower branches on the opposite side of the tree forced me to wait for a clear shot. By the time the buck came into the open, I was all shaken up! Frantically, I fired three more rounds as he disappeared around the hill. I never saw him again.

I had done my preseason scouting, prepared a stand, and picked out at least a dozen shooting lanes. Although I had mentally planned for about every possible scenario with which I might be presented, I wasn't ready. The Bible tells us that most people won't be ready when Jesus Christ returns. It's not that individuals won't have plans. However, their plans will be shortsighted. They will be concerned about the things of this life and not with the life to come. Jesus once said about His return, "Just as it was in the days of Noah, so also will it be in the days of the Son of Man. People were eating, drinking, marrying and being given in marriage up to the day Noah entered the ark. Then the flood came and destroyed them all" (Luke 17:26-27).

It's sad, but many hunters will devote much time thinking about where to hunt this fall, but little about where they will wind up spending eternity. However, God wants each one of us to be ready. The prophet Amos told the people of his day, "Prepare to meet your God" (4:12).

Prayer: *Lord Jesus, may You bring people to know You before it's too late. Thank You for the gift of eternal life and the opportunity to know the only true God. In Your name. Amen.*

Dr. Tom Rakow, Minnesota

OLD ANTLERS NEVER DIE . . . BUT THEY WILL BURN!
Scripture Reading: 2 Peter 3:1-14

A while back a friend of mine had a fire in his garage. Not only did Louis lose his building and the normal contents one would expect to find there, but he also lost his compound bow, portable tree stand, and (perhaps even tougher to take!) more than two dozen whitetail racks that were hung inside. Later, when he and family members sifted through the debris, they managed to find only a small chunk of one antler. Everything else had gone up in flames.

I have to say that this individual took it quite well. Better than I'm sure I ever would. Louis somehow managed to keep these material things, and even those with sentimental value, in their proper perspective.

Nevertheless, when you stop to think about it, every single antler will one day be turned into ashes. According to the Scriptures, there is coming a time when the entire physical world as we know it will be burned up. This will come about when Jesus Christ returns to judge the earth. The Bible tells us, "The heavens will disappear with a roar; the elements will be destroyed by fire, and the earth and everything in it will be laid bare" (2 Peter 3:10b). Yes, there is coming a time when all the physical things that we hold dear in this world will disappear.

Indeed, we need to realize that the material things of this world, which we so frequently allow to capture our affection and hard-earned currency, are quickly fading away. Are there certain items that you would really hate to loose? Whether we like it or not there is coming a time when every rifle, bow, boat, cabin, car, and truck will eventually be dissolved. This fact should have a powerful effect upon encouraging us to live in a manner which is pleasing to God. As Peter challenged his readers, "Since everything will be destroyed in this way, what kind of people ought you to be?" (2 Peter 3:11a).

Prayer: *Lord Jesus, help me to live for what is eternal. Amen.*

Dr. Tom Rakow, Minnesota

A PSALM IN LIVING COLOR
Scripture Reading: Psalm 42

I have read the book of Psalms many times during my life. Each year I participate in a daily Bible reading program that takes me through the entire Bible. I know, then, that I have used my eyes to read the book of Psalms at least a dozen times. The reason I mention this is that I actually saw a Psalm with my physical eyes. Confused? Let me explain.

One summer, my dad and I stopped at a bridge that crosses a local creek. We had stopped to cast our line a few times and try to catch a couple of Northerns. As we were walking down the bank, rod and reel in hand, I looked up, and about a hundred yards downstream was a doe lifting up her head from getting a drink of water.

That scene is like a snapshot in my mind. A solitary deer, gathering a drink of water in the midst of a stream, surrounded by bright green lily pads, a perfectly clear, blue sky overhead, and a backdrop of thick woods. The picture I viewed that summer morning was Psalm 42:1 in real life. It was a Psalm in living color. "As the deer pants for streams of water, so my soul pants for you, O God." That portion of Scripture came alive for me that day. It also encouraged my soul to continue thirsting for God, to know Him, and to watch for Him every moment.

Prayer: *Lord God, help me to seek You with all my heart. I ask this in Jesus' name. Amen.*

Doug Anderson, Minnesota

Devotions for Deer Hunters

ARE YOU THE PROVIDER?
Scripture Reading: Luke 12:27-31

For a long time, hunting was about the most important thing in my life. I always counted the days until deer season opened. In order to be able to hunt for a longer period of time, I eventually took up bowhunting. Even during high school, sports were of no real interest to me because they only interfered with hunting.

When I got married, my wife became a hunting widow. Many times I left her for the woods, and all the time I justified my behavior by telling myself and her that I was only trying to be a "good provider." It wasn't that I was unsuccessful. However, I didn't want to waste an opportunity to hunt. Even after my children were born, many a day and evening my wife cared for the kids while I played the "provider" role.

One day while I was in my tree stand, I suddenly realized that while I was trying to be the "provider," in fact I was just the opposite. Instead of being the father to my children and husband to my wife as God had intended, I was actually providing for my own selfish desires. I decided it was time to set my priorities straight: God, wife, family, self.

I wish I could tell you that it was easy, but it wasn't. In fact, I still struggle against the old sinful nature. Nevertheless, God has truly blessed me in every way. Even though I spend only a small fraction of the time hunting that I once did, I have never had my freezer so full of game!

Prayer: *Heavenly Father, thank You for Your promise of blessings to those who seek You first. Help me to keep my priorities straight. I ask this in Jesus' name. Amen.*

Ken Koch, Minnesota

HE NEVER CHANGES!
Scripture Reading: Malachi 3:6-12

We live in a changing world. As responsible deer hunters, there is a need to keep ourselves informed on ever-changing rules and regulations.

Today, many states are able to enjoy a plentiful deer herd. This is due in part to changes in land use and management.

And the equipment used for harvesting deer has also changed. This is true with regard to ammunition and firearms as well as archery equipment.

Even changes in the clothing hunters wear has come full circle. The standard red of years ago is now against the law in some states. We even have specialized camouflage patterns created to blend in with almost any type of background.

But, we can rest assured that God does not change. In the Old Testament book of Malachi, the Bible says, "For I am the Lord, I do not change" (3:6a). And in the New Testament book of Hebrews, we're told, "Jesus Christ is the same yesterday, today and forever" (13:8). If we are willing to let God change our hearts and choose Jesus Christ as our personal Lord and Savior, He will not only transform our lives, but He will also give us eternal life.

Prayer: *Lord God, thank You for remaining the same in the midst of change. Help me to be more like You. I ask this in Jesus' name. Amen.*

Jerome Jasken, Minnesota

THE LIE
Scripture Reading: Ephesians 4:25-28

When I was about ten, I attended a Billy Graham crusade with my father and brother. I went forward and publicly confessed Christ as my Savior. Although I believe I came to know the Lord at that point, I really didn't start to live for Him. I went through two divorces and a long siege of alcohol and drug abuse.

Then at the age of thirty-five or so, I rededicated my life to the Lord, and my life changed dramatically.

Eventually, I was invited to deer hunt with a group of Christians. My close friend Steve had an antlerless permit and requested that no one make an attempt to fill it for him until late in the day. However, soon after sunrise, two doe paraded past my stand and, despite Steve's desire to fill his own tag, I made the decision to fill it for him.

A short time later, Steve showed up. He had heard the shot and hoped I had a deer. I struggled with how to tell him that I had shot a doe. A doe that now desperately needed his antlerless tag! Thus the lie: "Steve, you wouldn't believe it! A buck and a doe came out and stood side by side in front of me. My shot missed the buck and dropped the doe!"

Steve was excited for me anyway and helped drag the deer out. Later that morning, a significant amount of time was also spent driving a swamp where the imaginary buck had disappeared. Not only had I lied to one of my best friends, but also to the rest of the hunting party. My lie had quickly grown.

Months passed, and I knew that I had to tell Steve the truth. As I sat before him and shamefully shared "the lie," Steve graciously forgave me and assured me of his continued friendship.

Through Steve I got a glimpse of what God's unconditional love for each of us is like. The Bible says, "But

God demonstrates his own love for us in this: While we were still sinners, Christ died for us" (Romans 5:8).

Prayer: *Lord God, thank You for loving us even when we are not very loveable. In Jesus' name. Amen.*

Les Stroklund, Minnesota

CONFESSIONS OF A POACHER
Scripture Reading: Psalm 51

Stepping out of the county courthouse, my eye caught something suspicious. There, next to the car, stood a stranger examining the deer tied to my trunk. A troubling thought quickly surfaced, "What if it's the game warden?"

You see, the same whitetail I was transporting with an archery tag on its leg had actually been shot with a twenty-two caliber rifle the day before. The reason for coming to the courthouse was a way to cover up my wrongdoing. Having misplaced a portion of my archery license, I needed a duplicate. Now, with a replacement license in hand, the deer could be "legally" registered. However, the sight of this middle-aged man (who was evidently not a warden after all) pricked my already guilty conscience. The words of the wisdom writer rang true, "The wicked man flees though no one pursues" (Proverbs 28:1a).

Sadly, this was not the first, nor would it be the last, deer I poached. And, although many years have now passed since that incident took place, it's still hard to believe I could be so brazen.

Sin is covered in a lot of ways in our day. Sometimes it's the worker who calls in sick when he or she is not, the taxpayer who purposely fails to record extra income on their return, or the hunter who inappropriately fills that tag of a hunting companion.

Whatever the case may be, the fact is nothing is hidden from God's eyes. The Bible declares, "The eyes of the Lord are everywhere, keeping watch on the wicked and the good" (Proverbs 15:3). King David asked, "Where can I go from your Spirit? Where can I flee from your presence?" (Psalm 139:7) Indeed, nothing gets past God. He sees all! He hears all! He knows all!

But the good news is God is able to forgive *all* sin.

Even a murderer (such as King David) found grace in God's eyes.

Now, the fact is the Lord still has a lot of work to do in my life. I'm not perfect, but I am forgiven. And, if the Lord was willing to forgive me for a multitude of sins, He will also forgive you!

Prayer: *Lord God, thank You for the blood of Christ that covers our sins. Thank You for removing my transgressions "as far as the east is from the west" (Psalm 103:12a). Be honored in my life this day. I ask this in Jesus' name. Amen.*

Dr. Tom Rakow, Minnesota

A MATTER OF MOMENTS
Scripture Reading: 1 Corinthians 1:18-31

It was the most important decision I had made in my short life. And now, as an adult, I know I will never make another decision as important as that one I made when I was nine.

The memory of those moments remain vivid when one of the leaders of the Bible club helped lead me in a prayer of repentance and salvation. In a matter of moments in the basement of a church, along with a cousin and a brother, I accepted Jesus into my life. That day the three of us made the decision to claim Christ as our personal Savior.

As I think back on those moments, it doesn't seem possible that any nine-year-old could have the ability to make such a life-changing choice. But, I know by experience that it is possible. This is part of the beauty of the gospel of Jesus Christ. It is so simple and understandable that even a young child can comprehend its significance. Jesus said, "Let the little children come to me, and do not hinder them, for the kingdom of God belongs to such as these" (Matthew 19:14).

These thoughts have often come to mind when I sit in a deer stand anticipating those few moments of action when the trigger is pulled or the string of the bow is released and one hopes for success. And then a flood of joy sometimes runs through my heart when I contemplate that in those same moments, another hunter could be making a decision for Christ and experience the ultimate hunting success. Namely, the success that comes by taking possession of eternal life through Jesus Christ.

Prayer: *Heavenly Father, thank You for making the gospel so simple. Amen.*

Doug Anderson, Minnesota

DON'T BLOW IT!
Scripture Reading: Matthew 16:24-28

I was still-hunting up a logging road, the prevailing wind was in my face and deer sign was everywhere. It was a perfect day to still-hunt: wet leaves and an overcast sky with the occasional spitting of snow showers.

At midday I was halfway up the road when a nice eight-point buck descended off the top of a ridge. He headed toward the breeding scrape located where the old road and ridge met. When the buck stopped just before dropping onto the flat, I prepared to shoot, but a sapling blocked a clear shot. The buck stepped down out of view and forced me to move up the old road to a rise where I could clearly see the buck in easy shotgun range. Why I didn't shoot then I still can't say, but I believe I just forgot I had a shotgun and felt the need to close the yardage as if in bowhunting.

Moving to close the gap, the next section of road dipped down removing all visual contact. As I came up out of the road's depression, suddenly I was in full view of the rutting buck. I had focused too much on the trail and keeping quiet. I saw the buck as his head was coming up and his lips were curled back, sniffing my scent. The air was swirling, and the buck winded then spotted me! Emotion rushed upon me and screamed, "Shoot! He's about to break and you'll lose him!"

The buck spun around and headed across the overgrown logging road. Leading the deer too far, I fired two quick shots in front of the buck. My brain began yelling at my runaway emotions, "What are you doing? At this distance you should aim dead on!" So, swinging the gun sight onto the buck's chest, I followed the deer as he ran. Squeezing off a shot: Boom! A ten-inch diameter poplar took a direct hit as the buck ran between the tree and myself. The eight-pointer then disappeared across the logging road and down the tree-choked ridge. I kicked myself many times for blowing that hunt, but now I can laugh at it—almost. I may have missed the mark on that hunt, but one hunting trip I didn't miss out on was the hunt for eternal life through Jesus Christ. You also can find success in the ultimate of hunts, the one for eternal salvation.

Prayer: *Lord, thank You for Your promise that, "everyone who calls on the name of the Lord will be saved" (Romans 10:13).*

Gerry Caillouet, Ohio

GOD USES ALL THINGS FOR GOOD!
Scripture Reading: Romans 8:28-39

For twenty years I worked as a high school band director in New York State's public schools. Along with this, I enjoyed hunting, wildlife photography, and being a State Bowhunting Instructor. Although I had been a Christian for many years, it was not until the loss of my wife in a tragic automobile accident in 1991 that I truly began to devote my life to the Lord's work.

Nevertheless, it was this seemingly senseless loss that ended up being God's way of making it possible for me to pursue my life-long dream of deer and wildlife photography. The Bible states, "And we know that in all things God works for the good of those who love him, who have been called according to his purpose" (Romans 8:28). Not only has the Lord given me a beautiful, new Christian wife and family; but by turning my years of wildlife photography experience to video, I began to produce Christian hunting and wildlife art videos. After a lifetime of being in the woods observing animals (especially deer) at close range, something inside compelled me to want to start capturing them on film.

In fact, the more time I spend in the woods, the more I am totally in awe of the marvelous perfection found in God's creation. God has designed each animal with exactly the right equipment it needs and an instinctive knowledge to use what it has been given.

It is very exciting to see what God can do with a life once you totally give it over to Him!

Prayer: *Lord, may You be glorified in every area of my life. I ask this in Jesus' name. Amen.*

Dave Tripicianno, New York

Devotions for Deer Hunters

NEVER SATISFIED
Scripture Reading: Isaiah 55:1-2

I've been hunting deer for thirty-one years now. I've hunted them with a bow, a rifle, and a shotgun; but I was never able to get enough. Like my dad always said, "The only time I ever said "no" was when they asked me if I'd had enough." Montana, Wisconsin, Ada, Virginia, Lac Qui Parle, Hutchinson, and then some. Sunup to sundown, hunt hard, never stop, never satisfied. Hunt those deer, never big enough, go, go, go. Many deer harvested, big bucks, nice bucks, does, fawns.

Deer hunting changed for me in 1984. After years of success and never being satisfied, God filled the gap. He filled the hole in my heart that only He could fill. Not just for the moment, but forever.

Yes, I still hunt deer, but now there is peace. God hunts with me. He wants me to succeed. Jesus Christ made my deer hunting better. I have more joy in seeing others succeed, I see more beauty in the woods, and the deer are more beautiful. The Lord helps me keep things in balance, and my wife and children are happier, too.

Prayer: *Lord, thanks for blessing us with the opportunity to deer hunt. Thank You for balance, grace, and peace. May You be glorified in my life in every area. I ask this in the name of Jesus. Amen.*

Louis King, Minnesota

LET GOD BE YOUR GUIDE!
Scripture Reading: Psalm 32:8-11

On a late October afternoon this past bowhunting season, my friend and I headed for a local public hunting area to spend the last couple hours of daylight sitting in a tree and waiting for a deer to wander our way. It was a cloudy, very windy afternoon; and I decided to position myself on the ground near the point of a long grove of trees outside of which a deer trail comes to a fork. If a deer did happen to come out of the low lying area, it would make its way right toward me and come to the fork in the trail. At this point, the deer would need to decide whether to go to the right and into a bean field or to the left and continue following a trail running alongside the grove of trees in which I was positioned. Whichever direction the deer chose, I was sure to have a close and clear shooting lane.

I had barely positioned myself behind a large tree with surrounding underbrush when up walks an average-sized buck exactly as I had hoped would happen. He slowly walked right up to the fork and then promptly stopped. In order for me to get the clear, close shot, the buck needed to choose to go to the right or to the left. As I mentioned, it was a very windy day and evidently the deer caught my scent because after many obvious moments of indecision, he chose to turn around and go quickly and safely from where he had come, choosing neither the right nor the left.

Naturally, I was somewhat disappointed at the decision the deer had made. However, as I now think back on that evening, I believe God was teaching me a lesson. Often during our lives, we may come to a fork in the road and need to consider going to the "right" or to the "left." Well, after this hunting experience, God showed me there is one other choice. Perhaps you are at a time in your life and your walk with God that has reached a fork in the road, and you have had many moments of indecision about which direction to go. Choosing to go to the "right" or to the "left" during a time of indecision could be costly to your walk with God as it could have been costly to the life of the deer. Take time to pray and wait for God to give you clear direction. He may simply be wanting you to turn around and return quickly and safely from where you just came.

Prayer: *Heavenly Father, thank You for Your willingness to "be our guide even to the end" (Psalm 48:14). Help me to be sensitive to Your Spirit, Your Word, and Your people. In Jesus' name. Amen.*

Doug Anderson, Minnesota

GOD GOT MY ATTENTION
Scripture Reading: Matthew 6:5-15

One Sunday morning while attending a weekend designed for spiritual renewal, I recognized that I needed a Savior and turned my life over to the Lord Jesus Christ.

The next few days, I was walking on air. I couldn't put the Bible down; I was reading it every chance I had. Before I was saved, the Bible didn't mean anything to me. I didn't understand what it was about. However, after I accepted Christ, the Holy Spirit helped me see what I was missing.

Three days later, I took my small Bible and went bowhunting. Up in my tree stand, I read in John 14:13-14, "And I will do whatever you ask in my name." So, I asked God for a six-point buck. I didn't have time to close the Book when a buck came running at me from the field in front of my stand. I got my bow ready for a twenty yard shot. There he stopped broadside. My arrow hit both lungs. He ran eighty yards—I saw him drop.

Although the buck ended up being a five-pointer instead of a six-pointer, I didn't care. This all happened so fast I couldn't believe it. Needless to say, God got my attention real fast. It's been several years now, and God is in my life everyday, every minute; and I thank Him for all that He's done.

Prayer: *Heavenly Father, thank You for the privilege and power of prayer. Thank You for knowing what things I have need of before I ask. Help me to trust Your answers whatever they are—yes, no, or wait. In Jesus' name. Amen.*

Jeff Koss, Pennsylvania

Devotions for Deer Hunters

FAITH: AN ESSENTIAL INGREDIENT
Scripture Reading: Galatians 3:1-14

Every whitetail hunter exercises faith. In fact, when you stop to think about it, deer hunting requires an enormous amount of faith. This is true regardless of whether one hunts with a bow or a rifle.

The bowhunter trusts in the stand being used, string or cable pulled, and broadheads attached. The person using bow and arrow must also place a measure of faith in one's own ability to accurately judge distance and the anatomy of a deer.

Faith is a requirement for the rifle hunter as well. To hunt with a rifle requires faith in the firearm carried, the company producing the ammunition, and the area being hunted.

Yes, from the onset, when we first purchase our hunting license (which fails to come with a money-back guarantee!) until we kneel down to fasten the site tag, we use faith.

Salvation also requires faith. However, instead of placing our trust in a number of things, we put our trust entirely in one person—the Lord Jesus Christ. Our faith rests in what Jesus Christ has done for us on the cross, not in what we have done or can do for Him. If we could be made right with God by going through some ritual or performing some good deed, Christ would never have needed to come and die on the cross. As Paul reminded the Galatians, "If righteousness could be gained through the law, Christ died for nothing!" (Galatians 2:21)

Prayer: *Father, help me to be a person filled with faith in You. I ask this in the name of Jesus. Amen.*

Dr. Tom Rakow, Minnesota

POWDER AND PULL
Scripture Reading: James 5:13-18

Do your prayers reach heaven?

When I first started shooting my old recurve, I developed the nasty habit of not taking a full draw. I would pull the bow all the way back, but then relax the string just before release. As a result, my arrow often dropped short of its mark.

Then, somewhere I read that it was helpful to gradually increase the draw just before releasing as a way of compensating. This has helped, but there are still times when I slip back into my old habit.

It's sad to say, but sometimes our prayers are like arrows from partially drawn bows or powderless bullets. In order for them to reach their destination, they should have some powder and pull behind them.

In today's text we see that Elijah's prayers were neither half-hearted nor haphazard. He prayed specifically and with great determination. James informs us, "He prayed earnestly that it would not rain" (James 5:17). God yearns for our prayers to be like Elijah's. God doesn't want us to mechanically go through some ritual. Our prayers can, and should be, hot with desire and filled with faith.

Prayer: *Heavenly Father, forgive me for the times when I merely go through a ritual instead of crying out to You with all my heart. Thank You for Jesus who makes it possible to boldly approach the throne of grace. Amen.*

Dr. Tom Rakow, Minnesota

Devotions for Deer Hunters

DON'T FORGET THE LIGHT
Scripture Reading: 1 John 1:5-10

Early one bow season, I had targeted southeast Ohio's whitetail deer. The wooded hills of Wayne National Forest produced a good crop of acorns that fed the resident deer population. I had located a prime breeding area near a group of white oaks on the side of a flat ridge. With a tree stand placed between the oaks and the scrape, I figured the action would prove exciting, to say the least.

Having parked my car on the side of the road, I got ready by the dome light of the family station wagon. With sunrise less than an hour away, I needed to hurry. As I started off, I chose to walk in the morning darkness, leaving my flashlight stored in my daypack. Soon my eyes adjusted, and I was able to see a few feet in front of me.

I found the well-cleared trail at the base of the ridge I would be hunting and started to ascend. The trail was easy to follow until the vegetation became thicker, about a fourth of the way up. Somehow in the steepness of the hill and the tangles of growth, I lost the trail. I stopped and tried in my mind to retrace my progress. For one second I thought of pulling out my flashlight, but I was in a hurry and was sure I could find my way without the light.

Being sure I knew where the path was, I altered my course and pressed on, but in no time I was breaking through brush with no trail to make the way easier. Stopping again I chased away the idea of pulling out the flashlight. Now I was angry I hadn't used the light and had lost my way. So, off I went busting my way up to a clear cut almost at the top. The openness of the small clear cut allowed me to see just how far off to the right I had traveled. Then looking down I noticed a huge hole ripped in my brand new camo pants. Suddenly I was reminded that this was how I and many other Christians travel down the path of life. God's Word says in Psalm 119:105, "Thy Word is a lamp unto my feet and a light unto my path."

Just as I learned about using a flashlight on the trail to my tree stand, we should all learn the importance of opening the Bible each day before we venture into God's great outdoors.

Prayer: *Thank You for Your word, Father, that guides me in the darkest times. Amen.*

Gerry Caillouet, Ohio

SOMETIMES PRAYER BRINGS PLEASURE
Scripture Reading: Matthew 6:25-34

Over the years I've heard many deer hunters testify as to how they have prayed for deer to cross their paths while hunting. I thoroughly enjoy hearing those testimonies and truly enjoy seeing the excitement on the faces of these people who have received answers to prayer.

For some reason, I have just never been comfortable uttering that prayer. It's not that I have believed that God can't answer or that He won't answer the prayer, but more to the fact that I'm not a very confident shooter. I'm afraid I'll miss what God has placed in front of me. This past bowhunting season, however, I had a limited number of opportunities to hunt. One day, as it was getting late in the afternoon, I decided to sincerely utter a prayer to God and ask Him to at least let me see a deer. On this particular day, I was bothered with the thought of perhaps going the entire day without seeing anything. As I finished my brief prayer, I turned my body to gain a more comfortable position in the tree stand; and there she was, a beautiful doe nibbling away on the underbrush just out of shooting range. I have to admit I was very surprised, but I shouldn't have been since just an instant earlier I had whispered "amen" for that very prayer.

I spent the last hour of daylight being entertained by that doe plus her two fawns as they eventually made a complete circle around me, always out of shooting range, nibbling and eating and smelling their way through the woods. I don't think they ever saw me, but their sense of smell never let them completely relax. I left the woods that day happy and confident in the fact that God had heard and answered my prayer to see a deer. Not only that, but He kept them just out of shooting range as well!

Prayer: *Thank You, Lord, for caring about the seemingly small and insignificant events in my life. Your pres-*

ence reassures me and gives me confidence. Amen.

Doug Anderson, Minnesota

BUCK FEVER
Scripture Reading: Romans 8:1-11

I will long remember the opening day of my first deer season. A member of our hunting party kicked out a nice six-pointer to me which stopped broadside only yards away. You could not have asked for an easier shot.

However, for some reason I could not bring the rifle to my shoulder. Instead, I shot eight times from the hip hitting dirt and trees a few feet in front of me. I watched helplessly as the buck finally bounded out of sight.

This was my initial and (hopefully) most memorable experience with a severe case of the jitters commonly known as "buck fever." Perhaps there was a time when you had a touch of the fever yourself.

Those who are unfortunate enough to fall under the influence of "buck fever" have been known to do such strange things as: shout "bang! bang!," lever unfired rounds on the ground, and yell for a deer to stop without firing a single shot. I even remember reading of one hunter who downed his deer and then ran to put the tag on. He ended up with his deer, but two broken legs as well. In all the excitement he forgot he was in a tree stand more than fifteen feet off of the ground!

Nevertheless, as powerful as "buck fever" may seem, there is a force far stronger at work in our lives—an energy that frequently explodes and injures everyone with whom it comes in contact. This power that I'm referring to is not limited to a particular season of the year nor to a select group of people called "hunters." No, this destructive energy indwells and at times overrides every single member of the human race. Its name—the sinful nature.

But God has not left us helpless. He has provided a "helper." There is someone who will take up residence in our life and begin bringing the sinful nature under control. His name—the Holy Spirit.

If we have truly trusted Jesus Christ as our Savior,

the Holy Spirit dwells inside of us and seeks to help us live lives that are pleasing to the Lord. As the apostle Paul told the believers in Rome, "You, however, are controlled not by the sinful nature but by the Spirit, if the Spirit of God lives in you. And if anyone does not have the Spirit of Christ, he does not belong to Christ" (Romans 8:9).

Prayer: *Father, help me to walk in the freedom that comes from Your Spirit. In Jesus' name. Amen.*

Dr. Tom Rakow, Minnesota

THE BUG
Scripture Reading: Romans 3:9-24

Every year I look forward to the first weekend in November. When that first Friday evening of November arrives, it means my family and I pack up the minivan and drive up to Mora, Minnesota, for the beginning of the annual rifle hunting season. Now, I'm not a great hunter. In fact, as far as hunting skills go, I'm below average. But I look forward to being out in the woods, enjoying God's creation during deer season, and I learn something new each year.

The first weekend of November was approaching and all week long I had been anticipating the trip north. When I awoke Friday morning, however, I noticed just a twinge of a sore throat. I attributed this feeling to the dry air circulating within our house and continued the day with the normal routine. However, as the day progressed, I could feel myself succumbing to a "bug." In fact, by that evening, as we were enroute to my parent's home, I knew deep down inside, despite how hard I was fighting it, that opening day was in jeopardy.

Not only was opening day lost to a "bug," but so was the entire weekend. Yes, I did foolishly try to go out for a few minutes before sunset on that first day, but the fever, body aches, chills, and sore throat quickly turned me around and back to the house under the multiple layers of warm blankets that awaited me in the bedroom.

My family and I returned home from opening weekend. I went to the doctor and received antibiotics to kill the "bug" and spent the first couple days of the following week recuperating. I spent that week asking God why I had to be sick THAT weekend. Why not the next weekend or the weekend before or last month?

As I reflect back to that weekend and the following week, I realize how foolish I was feeling sorry for myself. I am extremely fortunate knowing Jesus Christ as my

Savior and give thanks to God for His many blessings in my life. I only had a "bug" which invaded my body for a couple days and then was gone, but we have all been bitten by the "bug" of sin which brings death. The Good News is that God has provided the perfect antibiotic, namely Jesus Christ.

Prayer: *Dear God, help me to be a witness to those around me invaded with the "bug" of sin. May others ask Jesus Christ into their heart as their personal Savior.*

Doug Anderson, Minnesota

THE UNEXPECTED
Scripture Reading: 1 Timothy 1:12-17

As I arrived at my friend's farm, an area I had hunted several times before, the rest of the party was showing up. It was clear and very crisp that mid-November morning as we stood quietly in the dark and discussed the "game plan" for the day.

Finally, we were off to our respective stands. Mine was due north 600 yards across a recently plowed cornfield. As I labored across the frozen furrows, I stumbled and fell in the darkness, trying to be quiet, only to repeat the last action in frustration! Was it all worth it? Would I even see a deer?

As I came to the edge of the plowing, I could see my familiar stand of about twelve oak trees that rose above the surrounding area on a small knob of grassland. Once in place, I stood next to three of the oak trees that gave me good cover from visual detection.

So I settled in for first light. As the sun rose, the wind was from the north, just what I wanted. Fifty yards to the north was a good-sized creek with a bridge crossing it. All I had to do was sit tight and wait for the deer to cross the bridge as they had done many times before.

As the sun continued to rise, I could see the pheasants scurrying along the field's edge as if on little railroad tracks. The squirrels were doing their normal chatter and acrobatic acts. The geese were flying off the nearby lake to go out to feed. As I sat and watched this panorama of God's beautiful creation, I wondered how some could say this all "just happened. . . there is no Creator, no plan, it all just happened!"

At about 8:30, my attention was drawn to the south as I gazed across 300 yards of swamp to the edge of a large wood lot. Then I saw it, the unexpected. It was a buck working along the woods coming to a fenceline that would lead him directly downwind of me some 200 yards.

As I watched him pick his way, I thought of my earlier trek across the plowing and how I had perspired. I thought I must stink to high heaven. He's going to wind me and be gone. As he came into my wind, I watched as he came to a dead stop. His head and ears went straight up and he was staring intently at me. Then the unexpected. He turned north and came directly at me. In fact, he was prancing along at a good pace. As he approached the stand of oaks, about fifty yards out, he veered to my right down to the edge of the swamp. I thought, "Oh no, he's headed for the swamp, and I'll never see him again." But then the unexpected! He appeared next twenty-five yards to my right in an opening in the brush. He stopped and looked out across the swamp. I lifted my gun, pulled the trigger, and the unexpected was mine!

Over the past years, I've often wondered what caused that buck to do what he did that morning. He went against everything you would think he would do. He came upwind to a hunter he could smell. I guess I'll never know.

Another thought that comes to mind is of a young man broken down by life's disappointments—weighed down by guilt of past experiences in the world. The future had no apparent hope. The stink and filth of a life lived in immorality and anger hung all about him.

Who would have anything to do with him? Who would walk next to him and extend their love? Then the Unexpected! "But God showed His great love for us by sending Christ to die for us while we were still sinners. And since by His blood He did all this for us as sinners, how much more will he do for us now that he has declared us not guilty?" (Romans 5:8-9a, LB)

Yes, the Lord Jesus Christ came to me in a time I didn't expect Him or even think I was worthy. You see you don't have to clean up first. Just come as you are and watch for the Unexpected!

Devotions for Deer Hunters

Prayer: Lord, help us to see and to feel Your great love and mercy that You pour out onto us. Help us to recognize the grace that You extend to us. And then, Lord, show us how much we need You in our lives. Amen.

Les Stroklund, Minnesota

THE MOOSE HUNTERS
Scripture Reading: Psalm 128

As my husband and I neared the portage to Malberg Lake, we saw another party at the landing. The two were impossible to miss dressed in blaze camo. When we landed, we noticed among the portage items long guns and long lenses on the cameras. After checking over each other's equipment followed by the normal curious looks, the casual conversation started. The father-son hunting team hit the jackpot in Minnesota's moose lottery. They were out on a once-in-a-lifetime hunt.

Yes, they had seen moose and wolf tracks. No, they hadn't gotten a shot off—yet. They had another seven days before they needed to break camp and head home. We wished them well as we continued deeper into the wilderness.

During the next few days, the father-son team kept coming up in our conversations. They had made quite an impression on both of us. We really wanted them to bag their moose.

Coming out five days later, we ran into them again! All of us were pleasantly surprised and took the time to find out what had happened over the past few days. They were as eager to hear of our adventures as we were to hear about their hunting successes.

The son explained they had seen a large cow walking the shoreline with her weanling. The disappointment showed in his face as he explained he didn't get off a single shot. The long-lensed camera was just out of reach. The son's disappointment was mirrored on the father's face. Both, however, were having the time of their lives! They were enjoying the BWCA (Boundary Waters Canoe Area) wilderness, the hunt, and, most importantly, each other's company.

As we left the fifty-something son and his seventy-ish father, we wished them every success for the remainder of their hunt and stay in the BWCA. They both smiled. The trip was already a solid success even if they didn't get their moose. I thanked God for the love of a father and son. I praised God that they could share this time together, enjoying creation and each other's fellowship.

Prayer: *Heavenly Father, remind me again to shine Your love on those closest to me. Thank You for family and for the opportunity to share with them what is precious to me. Not only the wilderness and the hunt, but most importantly the love You show to each of us through the death and resurrection of Your Son, Jesus Christ. Amen.*

Valinda Litfin, Minnesota

GOD NEVER MISSES
Scripture Reading: Hebrews 2:1-4

His thick beams, long tines, and heavy body made him the type of buck about which every deer hunter dreams. Yet, this was no dream. This was the real thing! The big bruiser accompanied by a couple of does was in an open field and headed straight toward me.

When the huge twelve-pointer turned broadside, I squeezed the trigger—BOOM! The slug zipped past. "How could I have missed?" Struggling to maintain my composure, I quickly levered in the next round. Then, just as the whitetail started to quarter away—BOOM! I missed again, and then again!

The truth is I've missed a lot of times in my life. Not only have I missed with rifles, shotguns, and bows, I have also missed morally. I deserve hell. I deserve the arrow of God's wrath. And that's a scary thought because God never misses. That's right, never!

In the Bible we are told about a bow that was drawn by no one special—and it's arrow released without a precise target in mind. Nevertheless, this particular arrow hit the bull's-eye. The Word of God states, "But someone drew his bow at random and hit the king of Israel between the sections of his armor" (1 Kings 22:34a). God was behind this bow. As a result, in one swift flight of an arrow, the wicked rule of powerful King Ahab came to an abrupt halt. And it happened even though Ahab had tried to disguise himself in battle. Furthermore, the fulfillment of a prophecy of God's judgment made by a man named Micaiah (1 Kings 22:28) and another pronouncement made by Elijah (1 Kings 21:19) was also set in motion.

You see, it seemed that Ahab had gotten away with many terrible things. We are told in the Scriptures concerning him that, "There was never a man like Ahab, who sold himself to do evil in the eyes of the Lord, urged on by Jezebel his wife" (1 Kings 21:25). However, judgment finally fell on this evildoer. Ahab, despite his protective armor and a clever disguise, could not escape God's judgment.

The fact is, apart from a personal relationship with Jesus Christ, no one can escape the wrath of God. As the writer of Hebrews asked, "How shall we escape if we ignore such a great salvation?" (Hebrews 2:3) But the Good News is that Christ has paid the price for our sin. Indeed, "Since we have now been justified by his blood, how much more shall we be saved from God's wrath through him!" (Romans 5:9). With Christ there is no need for worry.

Prayer: *Heavenly Father, thank You for sending Your Son "Jesus, who rescues us from the coming wrath" (1 Thessalonians 1:10b). Help me to remember the great price that was paid. In Jesus' name. Amen.*

Dr. Tom Rakow, Minnesota

GOD'S GRANDEUR
Scripture Reading: Romans 11:33-36

Hunting in our home state of Wyoming recently was, well, let's just say, an eye opening experience! But through it all, God was continually teaching us.

With regard to antelope season—we accidentally wrote down the wrong area number on our applications. We did get a license. However, it was for an area we knew nothing about. As it turned out, we were able to explore new parts of Wyoming; and God did give us our antelope.

During the regular deer season, we hunted every chance we got. Even though we didn't fill our tags, again we enjoyed God's creation.

Over the years since we started hunting as a couple (more than a decade ago), we have always had enough wild meat to carry us from one season to the next. But by now all that was left for us to harvest was elk. And, we needed the meat. It ended up being unseasonably warm—shirt-sleeve weather. We dropped off two hunting partners at the top of a ridge and then went below to see what they would chase out. As we sat side by side on the edge of some timber, out stepped a beautiful deer. It was a five-point buck (by Eastern count that's a ten-pointer!). He walked within yards of us and never knew we were there. Even though we ended up with an empty elk license, we had a beautiful memory!

By the way—God did provide. Three friends from Minnesota shared some of their meat with us as a gift of Christmas love.

Prayer: *Dear Heavenly Father, thank You for always finding new ways to share with us the grandeur of Your creations. In Jesus' name we pray. Amen.*

Chuck and Cynthia Parmely, Wyoming

DOES GOD CARE ABOUT ANIMALS AND BIRDS?
Scripture Reading: Luke 12:22-26

The first book of the Bible reveals how God went to all the trouble of preserving animals and birds from the flood in Noah's day by directing an ark to be built (Genesis 6-9). We also find in the New Testament that even such an insignificant creature as a little sparrow is important. Jesus told his disciples, "Are not five sparrows sold for two pennies? Yet not one of them is forgotten by God" (Luke 12:6).

It's interesting that, from early on, God gave the Israelites specific guidelines for how animals and birds were to be treated. These directives included such things as rest on the Sabbath (Exodus 20:10; 23:12; Deuteronomy 5:14), the way work was to be accomplished (Deuteronomy 22:10; 25:4), provisions of food to be left for wild animals (Exodus 23:10-11; Leviticus 25:6-7), and proper treatment of a bird with her young (Deuteronomy 22:6-7). The book of Proverbs made it clear that the way a man treated his animal was a reflection upon his true moral character, "A righteous man cares for the needs of his animal, but the kindest acts of the wicked are cruel" (Proverbs 12:10). Even the handling and use of game that had been harvested received comment. The inspired Scriptures state, "The lazy man does not roast his game, but the diligent man prizes his possessions" (Proverbs 12:27).

Although Jesus stated that His disciples were "worth more than many sparrows" (Luke 12:7) and that a man's value is greater than that of a sheep's (Matthew 12:12), He never released humans from their responsibility of proper stewardship over His creatures. He wants us to be wise stewards. God desires that those who have been made in His own image should govern His creation appropriately. It only stands to reason that the way to have a right relationship with creation is by first having a right relationship with the Creator.

Prayer: *Lord God, thank You for providing what is necessary in this world. Help me to hunt in a way that is honorable to You. I ask this in Jesus' name. Amen.*

Dr. Tom Rakow, Minnesota

Devotions for Deer Hunters

THE STORM
Scripture Reading: Matthew 11:28-30

In October of 1975, one of my lifelong dreams became a reality. I went on a deer and elk hunting trip in Montana's Absaroka Range of the Rocky Mountains between Livingston and Gardner, Montana.

The third day of the hunt started out picture perfect. The sun was shining through a partly-cloudy Montana blue sky. The temperature was about sixty degrees. My friend Lance, an athletic seventeen-year-old, the youngest member of our party, and I were side hilling high above Immigrant Creek on the west side of the ridge from our truck and camp. We spotted a group of elk which seemed only two or three ravines in front of us. As we moved in their direction, time seemed to slip away. By two o'clock in the afternoon, the sky had darkened; and it began to snow. In a very short time, the snow was almost knee deep. We decided to head back to our truck on the other side of the ridge. As we labored through the snow, it became very apparent that we were in a serious situation. I became very fatigued and started to question my ability to continue. Lance warned me of the dangers of stopping and encouraged me to press on.

As we trudged through the now almost waist-deep snow, I was ready to give up; but Lance continued to break trail and prompt me on. About an hour after dark, we came safely to the truck. While we drove down the mountain to our camp, I wondered if I had been alone, would I have made it out without Lance's encouragement and direction?

Perhaps you recently found yourself going through life on one of those seemingly beautiful, trouble-free days; and, by midday, you were in the midst of a storm and needed someone to lead you out. Jesus said 2000 years ago, "I am the Way, the Truth, and the Life..." (John 14:6). Call on Him today, and I know He'll lead you out.

Prayer: *Heavenly Father, thank You for Your presence in our life and Your help and direction during the storms of life. Amen.*

Les Stroklund, Minnesota

UNDESERVED BLESSINGS!
Scripture Reading: James 1:17

It was the opening day of deer season, not just any deer season, but my first deer season ever. I had been practicing and waiting for this day a long time. Because it was my first time hunting, my dad wanted to stay fairly close so he sat on the next ridge over from me that morning.

After sitting for a while, I picked up some movement from the corner of my eye. Looking over my shoulder, I spotted a small-racked four-point buck slowly heading my way. My twelve-year-old heart took off like a rocket!

The buck continued on its slow pace toward me and allowed me to actually stand up, turn completely around, and raise the gun to my shoulder. Even so, despite all that movement, the buck just kept walking.

When he finally did notice me, he stopped and stood broadside.

Now there was nothing between that young buck and my shaking gun barrel. Nothing, that is, except the cool morning air. I held my breath in order to get my body to be still. I pulled the trigger. . . .

The buck took off and ran past my dad who quickly got off a shot. The buck continued up the next hill a little ways and then tipped over.

Being a rookie, I figured that since the deer didn't go down when I shot that I must have missed him. Nevertheless, I soon found out different. When we looked over the deer, we discovered a large hole from my dad's 30-06 in the chest area and the smaller hole from my .243 right through the heart.

I was, and still am, more than a little amazed. Especially when I think about all of the movement that I made and how it seemed that I couldn't hold my gun steady. Looking back on the events of that morning, I am now convinced that my good fortune was really a blessing from God. I had only a couple of hours of experience and had moved so much to get into position that I surely did not deserve to get that deer. However, the Lord does not merely give us things because we have earned or deserve them. He sends us blessings based entirely on His love and grace.

There have been times when I have hunted hard. I have pushed myself to stay still and sit out in the rain or snow or cold and figured I deserved to get a deer for my hard work, but didn't. There have also been times when I have been on stand for only a few moments and have filled my tag.

Nevertheless, as it is with hunting, so it is with life. Things don't always make sense. We don't always get what we think we should and often we get things even though we have done nothing to deserve them. But that's the way the Lord works.

We need to realize that God has a plan for us and things do not always happen how or when we think they should. Indeed, the Lord blesses us according to His will.

Just as I did not deserve to get that buck that first morning, I have done nothing to deserve the other wonderful blessings in my life. Ultimately, everything that I have is a gift from God.

Prayer: *Lord, thank You for granting all the wonderful gifts that we don't deserve. Thank You for demonstrating Your love for us in that, "While we were still sinners, Christ died for us" (Romans 5:8).*

Steve Hoecherl, Wisconsin

WHERE HE LEADS I WANT TO FOLLOW
Scripture Reading: Psalm 23

I had spent spring, summer, and early fall acquiring land on which to hunt. I scouted, did just what I had read, and got the advice of seasoned bow hunters. Now I was about to put that knowledge into practice. This was my first full season as a bow hunter.

On my way to the woods, I had to walk through a picked soy bean field. I spent this time observing the edge of the woods and praying. I was about to enter an area where I had previously observed several deer feeding.

However, I sensed the Lord impressing upon me the need to hunt another part of the woods about which I knew little. I struggled, "Was this actually the Lord, or my own lack of confidence being a beginning bow hunter?" I followed the "impression" believing the Lord wanted to show me something. After all, part of my prayer was, "Show me where I am to hunt."

Because I was running out of daylight, I settled on the ground near some fallen logs. A few minutes later, a six-point buck came within my shooting range. Although time prevents me from explaining all that happened, I was able to take three shots—and was quite shook up in the process. I didn't get the buck, but believe that this hunt ended the way God intended it to end. Thinking back, that hunt impacted the rest of the season.

Eventually, I took a doe; and, if not for that hunt, it would have been a frustrating first bow season. But, as a result I've learned to listen to God when I hunt. Even though I won't harvest a deer every time, God is teaching me; and I must be open to Him and listen. The Lord is able and willing to lead us in every area of life. As the Lord spoke through the psalmist, "I will instruct you and teach you in the way you should go; I will counsel you and watch over you" (Psalm 32:8). Let's not limit God.

Let's let Him guide us when we hunt and in everything else we do.

Prayer: *Lord, help me to trust in You. Help me to understand when and where You are directing me, and help me have the faith to follow You.*

Jim Suttinger, Ohio

ELK HUNT
Scripture Reading: Numbers 9:15-23

It was my first archery elk hunt and my friend Kent and I were both excited. We drove my old, rusty van from Minnesota to Colorado and laid down a hefty price for a non-resident license.

A week earlier, a friend who lived in the area assured us that the elk were active on the mountain we would be hunting. Setting up camp at about 10,000 feet—we hunted down during the day and made our way back up the mountain at night. Nevertheless, after a couple of days of hunting it became abundantly clear the elk had moved out of the area. So, we began looking in other locations.

To be where the elk were we knew it was necessary to relocate. Although it didn't happen until we were on our way home—we did wind up spotting a few elk and plenty of fresh sign.

In the end, we both came back home without ever releasing an arrow at an elk. Nevertheless, there was something truly wonderful and refreshing knowing we were close to elk.

The Bible tells us that during the days of Moses the Israelites were able to follow a pillar of cloud by day and a pillar of fire by night. In order for the Israelites to be with God, they found it necessary to be where God wanted them.

When the Hebrews came out of Egypt, God guided them with a cloud. We are told, "Whether the cloud stayed over the tabernacle for two days or a month or a year, the Israelites would remain in camp and not set out; but when it lifted, they would set out" (Numbers 9:22). To be where God was manifesting His presence, they needed to move when and where God wanted them to move.

In the Bible, a believer's life is often described as a

walk. For example, John told his readers, "If we claim to have fellowship with him yet walk in the darkness, we lie and do not live by the truth. But if we walk in the light, as he is in the light, we have fellowship with one another, and the blood of Jesus, his Son, purifies us from all sin" (1 John 1:6-7).

The Christian life is also described as a race. Running in God's race requires us to "run with perseverance the race marked out for us" (Hebrews 12:1b). Friend, are you walking the walk and running the race?

You see, it's not God's desire that we live in the past where God has been at work. He wants us to walk close to Him right now. Some people turn to the traditions of the past. They think that if they attend a church where they grew up, or practice some long-standing ritual they will be all right. But the Bible never states this.

Friend, we are called to be doing what God wants us to do right now. We can't hide in the traditions of the past and then expect to experience God's presence in a powerful way. The God of the universe is a living God— not some lazy or lethargic deity. He is dynamic and powerful, not stagnant and stale.

Are you where God wants you to be? Are you (at this exact moment) doing what God is calling you to do? If not, step out in faith and follow Him.

Prayer: *Lord, help me to be dynamic like You! May others look at my life and be able to know that I am walking the walk and running the race for Your glory. I ask this in Jesus' name. Amen.*

Dr. Tom Rakow, Minnesota

Devotions for Deer Hunters

CLEARING THE BRUSH
Scripture Reading: Hebrews 12:1-2

Each year I go out in the woods early in the fall and check the conditions of my favorite deer stands. These are permanent wooden stands that periodically need some upkeep to keep them solid and safe. What surprises me more than the weathered condition of the stands, however, is the tremendous growth and thickness of the underbrush in the area around the stands and throughout the shooting lanes. Each year this thick growth of brush and briars which can trip, whip, tear clothing and skin, and entangle, keeps me from being able to clearly see the target that I desire to see which is, hopefully, a deer with a large set of antlers. So a lot of time is spent cutting and clearing the growth of brush and briars, opening the shooting lanes, and allowing for a much clearer view of the desired target. It is at this point that I think to myself, "Instead of clearing the brush just once a year, it should be done continuously, so that it doesn't have the opportunity to grow so thick and tall and become so undesirable."

And so it is with my Christian life and my relationship with Jesus Christ. When I allow the sinful desires of this life to so easily entangle me and I neglect to do anything about it, my relationship with Christ becomes overgrown. I then need to spend some time cutting and clearing the brush out of my life by repenting and asking God to forgive me of the sin which so easily entangles. The pathway to Jesus is then cleared, and the target I desire is much easier to see and to follow.

Prayer: *Heavenly Father, help me to "throw off everything that hinders and the sin that so easily entangles" (Hebrews 12:1). I ask this in Jesus' Name.*

Doug Anderson, Minnesota

WATER HOLES
Scripture Reading: John 7:37-39

"Hot and dry!" are a couple of words that could best describe the archery season that year throughout much of the midwest. Southerly winds, plenty of sun, and no rain brought day after day of fair skies and warm weather. This made for pleasant days afield, but wasn't helping deer movement, at least not in the hardwoods where I planned on hunting.

As I spent long hours in my stand, I felt hot, restless, and thirsty. "Thank God for water!" I remember thinking as I took a drink. The Psalmist wrote, "As the deer pants for streams of water, so my soul pants for you, O God" (Psalm 42:1). I wish I could say that describes me more.

I was hoping the deer were as thirsty as I was. There wasn't much water around. Most of the small creeks were dry. Only the ponds held a reliable source of water. The key would be finding the one the deer were using.

A water hole is a source of food, providing water for green shrubs, persimmons, and succulent grasses. It also serves as a constant stop-over for bucks in search of estrus does during the rut. And, because all deer, including large nocturnal bucks, need water more readily than food, it is not uncommon for them to visit the water source during daylight hours.

My brother and a buddy of his had noticed a lot of tracks at a pond earlier in the summer and had hung a stand there. By the looks of the sign, the time to hunt it was now. The water hole was in dense cover and situated near a milo field and a bean field. The deer were concentrated in this area as the abundance of tracks and trails indicated.

The first day I hunted the pond was one to remember. The temperature was in the low eighties, and the wind was perfect. I sat perched high above the water hole in my tree stand.

I watched as squirrels and birds made their way to the water's edge. It was 5:15 p.m. when the big buck emerged from his bed about fifty yards away. He came to the pond with his mouth open and tongue hanging out. What a sight it was to watch him take long drinks at the water's edge.

He came directly below my stand unaware of my presence. That is until I shot and missed. I shook my head in disgust as one of the nicest bucks I had ever hunted retreated into the dense thicket from which he had come. I was sorry I had shot and missed him. Another mistake, another lesson learned! Learning is a part of each hunt for me.

By the way, when was the last time you thanked God for water? The next time you are hunting a water hole you might remember to thank the Lord. After all, without water we wouldn't be here. The fact is, in many countries when an individual asks for a drink, they hope for clean water; but any water will do. Every last drop will be swallowed because there is none to spare. Can you imagine what an ice cold glass of milk or an ice cold soft drink would taste like to someone who has never had such a treat?

That is exactly what Jesus is like to a thirsty soul. He is like a fresh spring of water that never goes dry. He is a constant source of strength. Much like the deer count on that one source of water, you too can count on Jesus to be there. But unlike some ponds, He always has something to offer. He will be there when all other things you lean on are long gone.

Jesus offers living water, eternal life, to anyone who is thirsty, for anyone who will come to drink. Come to Him. He promises you won't be denied.

Prayer: Lord Jesus, thank You for Your promise of

"living water" (John 4:10). Help me to direct those who are thirsty to You. Please make me a channel of blessings to others. In Your Name. Amen.

Troy Peterson, Missouri

PIECES AND PARTS
Scripture Reading: 1 Corinthians 13:11-12

After several years of hearing about my dad's deer hunting exploits, the day finally came when I could accompany him into the woods. Though I did not carry a rifle at first, I learned many lessons from him during those times. Safety was his first concern. "All of the deer in the woods are not worth a man's life," he would repeat each hunting season.

One basic lesson he taught me was that I should not expect to see the complete deer. "Look for legs, or an ear, or lateral objects, or anything else which would stand out from the other scenery among the trees, brush, and tall grasses in which we hunt." Basically he was saying, "Look for pieces and parts." If I studied deer so well that I knew almost everything about them, I could identify something as being a deer just by catching a glimpse of one part of the whole creature.

This relates directly to how we handle our walk through life once we have invited God to reign in our lives. We won't understand the whole essence of our existence until time has passed and hindsight lets us see the joys and struggles more fully. If we want to know how God is working in our lives, we need to know Him in a very detailed manner: read His Word, fellowship with other believers, and spend time in prayer with Him.

Then look for the pieces and parts of our daily life in which we can see and/or hear God's working through us. Count your blessings, then notice how many or all of them have led you to a point in your life where God's purpose for things of the past have now come to fruition.

My dad's lessons on deer have made my hunts more enjoyable by allowing me to see more deer in the woods. Observing God working in your life, in even small ways, will improve your sighting pieces of the whole picture— the whole God who loves you and wants to abide within you.

Prayer: Lord God, help me to recognize Your presence by the "pieces and parts" You allow me to see. I ask this in Jesus' Name. Amen.

Michael Herman, Wisconsin

AN INVISIBLE WOUND
Scripture Reading: Psalm 32:1-5

    I had a painful experience during a recent deer gun season. It wasn't a bodily injury sustained on the hunt, but rather a form of mental anguish as the result of a careless act.

    The deer population in my old stomping grounds (the farmlands of western Wisconsin) was at an all-time high. This territory is shotgun only and the opening weekend is fairly quiet with most hunters content to stand. However, by mid-week the neighbors get together to "push the woods." Needless to say, by the second weekend many of the deer are on the move.

    I'm not a good snap-shooter, nor am I very good on running deer. My old Ithaca might be good for grouse, but I've always questioned its consistency at throwing slugs straight. By the Saturday following Thanksgiving, I had missed no less than three deer under such conditions.

    After lunch that day, our little group banded together to hunt a neighbor lady's land. This familiar tract of ground had been trodden upon numerous times by myself and friends Kevin, Dave, and his boy Justin. We got permission from our host whose house sits on the edge of the woods. The first drive was uneventful so Kevin and I volunteered to make the final push on a hilltop above the house.

    Finishing the drive, I met up with Justin who had been waiting patiently. Meanwhile, Kevin continued on in order to hit a remote corner of brush a bit beyond where the drive ended.

    We were on our way back to the vehicles—about one hundred yards from the house—when Justin and I heard shots ring out on the hilltop above us. Sure enough, Kevin rousted a wide-racked buck past Dave which he found difficult to get in his scope. Two rounds hurried the deer our way.

Justin was behind me when the big antlered buck hit a small opening forty yards ahead. I quickly raised the pump and got off a single shot. As quickly as the buck appeared, he was gone. But my mind was left spinning in horror. However, not because I had missed, but because I had just broken one of gun safety's foremost rules. In the heat of the moment, I had lost my composure and shot in the direction of a very familiar house. The home was situated just beyond some small pines and brush in front of which the deer had crossed. Call it a fleeting lapse of judgment, nerves being rattled, or plain old-fashioned buck fever. I had thrown caution to the wind, and now all I could envision was looking through a busted window at an elderly woman lying on her living room floor in a pool of blood. The fact that a youngster had seen all this unfold over my shoulder only added to the shame. I confessed to all what a stupid thing I had just done. The guys tried to reassure me that a slug wouldn't make it through the twigs and pine boughs intact to cause any damage.

We examined the house's siding for a hole made by the slug and found none. I was grateful things hadn't turned out worse, but was still shaken.

In a similar way, there have been many times in my life when I have either missed or opposed God's will by making an impulsive decision. I have made quick choices that resulted in cruel or harsh words and thoughtless actions—the kind of sin which the apostle Paul summed up in Romans 7:15 by saying, "I do not understand what I do. For what I want to do I do not do, but what I hate I do."

We need God's help in order to keep us from making destructive decisions. As we look to the Lord, He will give us guidance and clear thinking at all times.

Prayer: *Lord God, may Your Holy Spirit control all my*

actions at all times. Keep me from making dangerous and destructive decisions. I ask this in Jesus' Name. Amen.

Gregg Wheeler, Wisconsin

SHOULD I OR SHOULDN'T I?
Scripture Reading: Joshua 24:14-15

Well, here I was on the first day of the new year and the last full day of the season up in an old pine tree, sitting at the edge of a beautiful cypress swamp located near the Florida Everglades. The spot was in some of the most active scrape area I had seen in a long time. As I sat there in my climber tree stand, I began to realize how good God had been to me. I didn't really care if I shot anything or not, so about 10:30 a.m. I put my bow in its rest and began to praise Jesus (quietly!). I said, "Lord, just being here with You and enjoying what You have given us is enough. My cup runneth over. What more could You do?"

Suddenly, a sound came up behind me from the ground below, and it sounded large! I thought, "Lord, You have given me the desires of my heart, and now You are doing more?" Turning slowly and picking up my bow, I got set to draw. I looked down in the palmetto bushes and saw a large, black object which I determined to be about 350 pounds. "It must be a boar hog," I said (quietly to myself). But then, much to my surprise, out walked a BIG black bear and stood broadside to me about twenty yards away. I almost fell out of my tree stand! I had never seen a black bear while hunting, and the excitement was overwhelming.

Now it's doubtful that anyone in this 48,000 acre management area would have ever known if I had harvested that bear. But knowing it was illegal, the bear was left to walk by. Furthermore, the Bible says, "There is nothing concealed that will not be disclosed, or hidden that will not be made known" (Luke 12:2).

What I want to say is that whether we are young or old, our life is full of choices. The choices we make affect our future. Therefore, it is important that we choose wisely. Make the right choice even if no one is around, and please make the right choice and accept Christ into your life!

Prayer: *Lord Jesus, help me to make choices that honor and please You.*

Rev. Ed Dedmon, Wisconsin

LITTLE THINGS
Scripture Reading: Psalm 104:10-25

It is dark and the forest is still as I climb and then sit in my stand. Taking a deep breath, the cool, crisp air pours into my lungs and seems to cleanse me to the core.

I love the woods in the early morning when the sun begins to rise and transforms the shadows into light. The new day begins with the wind rustling through the remaining leaves, the birds start to sing and fly while squirrels and other creatures scurry about. All of these little ordinary things happen every day. They go on whether I am out here or not. But on this particular day, I am fortunate to witness it all. Yes, whether I am on my stand, at work, or at home—these things still happen. Everyday, God displays the wonders of His creation in the simplest of ways.

Too often it seems that we don't have or don't take the time to observe. Unfortunately, the beauty of a sunrise, sunset, or starlit night all too often go unnoticed. But the little gifts that God gives us are not only found in nature, they exist everywhere in our daily lives. Our family, our friends, our health, our jobs, our food and shelter, along with all the material items that make our lives more enjoyable, are all gifts from God—gifts which can be taken for granted.

Let's take time to thank and praise Him. As the writer of the book of Hebrews admonished, "Through Jesus, therefore, let us continually offer to God a sacrifice of praise—the fruit of lips that confess his name" (Hebrews 13:15).

Prayer: *Thank You, Lord, for all of Your blessings, big and small!*

Steve Hoecherl, Wisconsin

Devotions for Deer Hunters

MAKE YOUR SHOT COUNT!
Scripture Reading: Philippians 3:12-14

It was a good deer stand with a great view. I was up about ten feet in a clump of three trees located on a little rise from which you could peer through and over the thick brush and scrub poplars and on out to the swamp. My uncle and my boys were making a sweep through the woods. They were on the other side of the swamp to the north and northwest of where I was positioned. Rayburn (my cousin's husband) was also nearby on a stand just over a knoll.

As they drove the woods, I heard the step, step, step noise of a deer walking ahead of them. The noise of the foot steps changed to a slight sucking noise as the deer proceeded across that arm of the swamp and then back to the dry. The whitetail was getting closer!

Suddenly there she was, a beautiful, healthy doe walking along as if taking a Sunday stroll through a clearing some sixty yards away. I tried to contain my excitement. She was broadside—a perfect shot opportunity. Taking the old military 30.06, I focused the cross hairs of the scope on her vitals—and fired. That doe just kept right on walking like nothing had happened. She went up the slope between Rayburn and me so that I didn't dare take a second shot. Moments later, I discovered that a second shot would have been out of the question anyway because I had simply jacked the empty shell half out—and then right back into the breech.

Why didn't I hit the target? Well, I was to blame. I wasn't as familiar with my dad's old 06 as I thought I was. I should have spent time out on the practice range. Then there was also the excitement—the buck fever (or in this case doe fever!). It makes you do strange things.

So it is with our lives. We either pick the wrong target, or we wind up neglecting the fundamentals of life and thereby overlook what is truly important. Instead, let's follow the apostle Paul's example and focus on "the goal to win the prize" (Philippians 3:14). Let's focus on Christ!

Prayer: *Lord Jesus, make my aim Your aim, my will Your will. Amen.*

Chaplain Dan Holmes, Minnesota

Devotions for Deer Hunters

ALL THINGS ARE POSSIBLE
Scripture Reading: Mark 11:20-26

My brother spotted the large-racked buck, big doe, and a decent eight-pointer out in the middle of an open field. The snow was deep on that stormy December afternoon. And, to my brother (who would die in a car accident a few months later), the huge fourteen-pointer and the whitetails with him must have seemed unapproachable. Anyway, that's the only way I can explain his choice not to pursue this exceptional trio.

The flurries were heavy as I cut a path up the steep hill and then onto the tree-covered ridge which was above and behind the field where the three deer were. Walking out a point—I stopped. I could hear my brother yelling from the busy highway below, "Turn around! Turn around!"

As I turned, my eye caught site of the massive-racked fourteen-pointer charging up the hill some fifty to sixty yards behind me. I quickly pulled back my thirty-pound recurve and launched the arrow with an arc that resembled that of an English longbowman in battle. Although I never should have shot, the excitement proved too much.

Now, as you might have guessed, I missed that monster buck (which thirty plus years later still remains the largest I've ever seen). Nevertheless, just the fact that as a fourteen-year-old boy I got closer than most hunters still serves as a lasting source of encouragement. Yes, some things are worth trying—even when it may seem entirely useless to do so.

How much more should we attempt or ask for the impossible when serving the Lord? Jesus even encouraged His followers to exercise faith by saying, "Everything is possible for him who believes" (Mark 9:23b). And again, "All things are possible with God" (Mark 10:27b).

Friend, let's trust God for the impossible! Let's step

out in faith! After all, "Without faith it is impossible to please God, because anyone who comes to him must believe that he exists and that he rewards those who earnestly seek him" (Hebrews 11:6).

Prayer: Lord Jesus, help me to believe You for the impossible! I ask this in Jesus' name. Amen.

Dr. Tom Rakow, Minnesota

GO INTO ALL THE WOODS
Scripture Reading: Matthew 28:19-20

As the slug season approaches again here in Ohio, I am reminded of the untimely death of a hunter I knew that happened last slug season. He died while hunting, although it wasn't a hunting accident. Unfortunately, I am fairly confident that my friend died outside of the grace of God.

I pondered the thought of spending one year of total separation from God without the hope of ever having redemption. After one year it's only the beginning of an eternity of utter hopelessness and total damnation. Consider this and dwell on it for a minute thinking of someone you know who has not experienced the salvation Christ freely offers. It's very sobering.

Think back over the times you have been hunting and consider the number of hunters you have encountered. How many of them are saved? Only God knows. However, there is something you could do about it, and it's in your hands right now. Purchase some extra copies of this book and give them to hunters or leave them in bow and gun shops. God will, and is, using this book to reach hunters for Christ. You can offer hope to hunters who might have none.

Prayer: *Lord Jesus, help me to be sensitive to the Holy Spirit and reach out to other hunters. Give me the words to say and courage I need. Amen.*

Jim Suttinger, Ohio

HIS EYE IS ON . . . .
Scripture Reading: 1 Peter 5:6-7

The miracle of birth is an amazing thing in all creatures, and deer are no exception. Though I have been involved in raising deer for over a dozen years, I have only been fortunate enough to watch one doe give birth. For the past three years, I have been trying to capture the birth of a fawn on film. With several does in my deer herd from which to choose, I didn't think it would be difficult to find one going into labor. I was wrong!

I watched and waited for signs from any of them that the big moment might be near. I could tell most were very close so I was prepared with the camera and spent many hours just sitting, waiting. When it seemed nothing was happening, I would take a break and return minutes later to find two babies on the ground next to mom.

As I reflect on how difficult it is for me to know the exact moment of birth, I am reminded that God knows when each "doe bears her fawn" (see Job 39:1). This is just one more example of the awesome power of God. If He knows about each deer in the forest and keeps track of all the sparrows, just think of how much He cares about you!

Prayer: *Heavenly Father, thank You for watching over what we cannot. Thank You for taking care of all that You have created. Indeed, "The eyes of all look to you, and you give them their food at the proper time. You open your hand and satisfy the desires of every living thing" (Psalm 145:15-16).*

Caara Holmstrom, Minnesota

A RED FLAG
Scripture Reading: Acts 17:24-28

When I was in college, I was majoring in biology with the dream of one day becoming a Wildlife Biologist. I hoped to work for a Fish and Wildlife Department with lots of opportunities to fish and hunt game which I would never have the chance to pursue in my home state of Maryland. Before I transferred to the University of Maryland, I attended Prince George's Community College to bag many of the requirements I would need. It was in my Biology 101 class that a major turning point in my belief system started to take what would become a 180 degree turn. We were learning about the way life just suddenly happened billions of years ago. No one had to sell evolution to me as I came to college already a believer of "this scientific truth." I was not a believer in God.

When we arrived at natural selection, for the first time a red flag went up in my mind. My professor explained that 99.99% of all mutations were detrimental to the species. In other words, when an offspring is born with physical change from the parents, it is going to die! That meant that only .01% will live. Our teacher was able to give several examples of defects that caused the newborns to perish, but only one of a mutation that was a benefit. But was it?

The professor related a story of a farmer in England who had a lamb born with very short legs. So, he bred a variety of short-legged sheep so farmers wouldn't need fences that were high. "Wait a minute!" I thought. I was a hunter and right away pictured big horn sheep in my mind. A short-legged lamb would be the first one a cougar would catch when an attack on a flock occurred. In the wild this wasn't a benefit so the mathematical percentage to me seemed to point against evolution. The seeds of doubt were planted and began to grow.

Prayer: Lord God, thank You that all truth points to You. Keep me from falling prey to the lies and false philosophies of humans. I ask this in Jesus' name. Amen.

Gerry Caillouet, Ohio

Devotions for Deer Hunters

ADJUSTMENTS
Scripture Reading: Matthew 18:1-4

This year I spent more time getting ready than I usually do. Two years ago I bought a different bow because it seemed I should have more let off. However, with the newer bow, my shooting was not consistent. So, I got a book in order to know how to make the proper adjustments.

The bow string frayed when I was getting measurements—so that meant getting a new bow string. It was also recommended that I use a different rest. I decided to switch, and that meant either replacing the nocks on the arrows to a different position or getting new arrows with nocks already in the right position. My son had some carbon arrows, and I thought they looked nice so I decided to get new carbon arrows.

I tried to paper tune my shots, but couldn't get it until my son wanted to shoot it. He had a different type of release. And, when I used his, the paper tuning was fine. But that meant I needed to get a different release. What a process to make sure everything is as it should be!

Then God spoke to me about how much I did to get ready for the season—how much time I had spent getting everything in order. He reminded me that there were times when I did not have things in order for Him. Indeed, we sometimes make God settle for less than our best—when we should be making some necessary changes.

Prayer: *Lord, help me to always give You my best. Help me to make the adjustments in my life that need to be made in order to bring You honor and glory. In Jesus' name. Amen.*

Kent Rydberg, Minnesota

KEEP IT SIMPLE
Scripture Reading: Romans 10:13-15

We live in a high-tech society—there's not much doubt about that. Just take a look at people the next time you are running errands around town. Or perhaps take a look at yourself. It won't take long before you notice people armed with cell phones, pagers, palm pilots, and various other gadgets in their hands or strapped to their waist.

It seems as if all parts of our lives are becoming technical and complex, even our hobbies and activities we do for enjoyment. Collecting and trading baseball cards used to be a simple hobby for kids, but now it has become so high-tech that it is nearly impossible for a person to keep up with all the trade magazines, catalogs, CDs, and other forms of information that are out there for the simple collector. Deer hunting, of course, is no different. Going into one of the large hunting stores these days, a person can be overwhelmed with the technology and information available to the hunter. There is enough stuff out there to saturate even the heartiest of hunters. Technology has become a part of the equipment, the strategy, and even the clothing one wears.

For me, when a hobby or area of interest I enjoy becomes highly technical and complex, the enjoyment begins to recede. It becomes more work than fun. When I play softball, I don't want to read all of the latest trade magazines and catalogs to determine which bat and glove I should be using this season. When it comes to deer hunting, I love to read about people's hunting experiences and what made their hunt successful; but I'm not all that interested in the statistics and technology of the gun or bow that was used to take the deer.

I do realize the importance and necessity of science and technology in our world today, but I need things explained to me in simple terms. That's one reason I love

God and His word. When it comes to inheriting eternal life, God made the message simple. In Romans 10:13, God says, "For whoever will call upon the name of the Lord will be saved." I love simple messages. It is not necessary for me to have to understand and keep up with the science and technology that documents the accuracy of God's Word although I understand it is important. For me, it's only necessary to keep it simple and understand that God loves me; and that through calling upon the name of the Lord in repentance and forgiveness of my sins, I have the assurance of eternal life. My hope is that you, too, will keep it simple and call upon the name of the Lord today.

Prayer: *Dear God, thank You for the simple message of God's love. I thank You for technology, and for the people who are able to use it in furthering the spread of the Good News. Help me to be aware of the necessity of technology, but keep Your message of salvation simple.*

Doug Anderson, Minnesota

BEING THANKFUL
Scripture Reading: Philippians 2:1-4

A couple of years ago I was given the opportunity to hunt on some private land by a fellow Christian church member. Being fairly new to the area as well as being financially strapped, I wasn't left with a choice of great places to hunt.

Furthermore, all I had left was a twenty-gauge to use for a deer hunting weapon. My personal choice had always been a scoped bolt-action 270 with a zippy 130 grain bullet. I previously had two such beautiful specimens. However, I ended up selling them to pay bills.

Not only had this generous friend allowed me to bow hunt on his land, but he was also so gracious that he allowed me to gun hunt with him. In addition, he allowed me to borrow one of his deer rifles, a scoped 270. Praise the Lord!

At about 8:45 opening morning, I selected a nice buck from a group of does silently filtering through the heavily brushed area near me. One shot rang out from the loaned 270.

Waiting twenty minutes, I climbed down and followed the blood trail one hundred yards or so to the most beautiful ten-point I have ever harvested! Thankfully, with a tear in my eye and praise for the Creator, I knelt down and thanked the Lord for His gifts, His presence, His grace, and (you better believe) my compassionate friend Bill!

Prayer: *Lord, help me to daily be thankful for all Your gracious gifts! In Jesus' awesome name. Amen!*

Robert W. Acker, Wisconsin

Devotions for Deer Hunters

ARE YOU COMFORTABLE WHERE YOU ARE?
Scripture Reading: Psalm 84:10-11

If there is one thing I have noticed in my years of hunting, being comfortable and confident always makes for a more productive hunt. I have seen many new elk hunters travel out west and settle for what seemed like a good spot—when just over the hill was fresh sign.

Some of the most successful hunters I know spend much more time scouting than they do actually hunting. Their percentage of success speaks for itself!

Recently I found a spot and began hunting. But, something wasn't right. Was this the best place I could be? I had a nagging feeling inside and couldn't sit still. Was this really the best place to be spending valuable time? How would I ever know unless I got up and started scouting. I scouted about four hours before I found a spot I felt comfortable in hunting. I now could have confidence in my position, and the long wait paid off with a good bull!

Are you comfortable in your heart? Or, have you settled for a lifestyle short of what God desires? You can never feel comfortable until you are in the place God wants you to be. Indeed, there will always be an inner emptiness unless you fill that void with Jesus Christ. Don't waste time being unproductive. After all, God has a plan for you. Just seek His will.

Prayer: *Dear God, I often settle for less than Your will for my life. Help me to be all that You want me to be. I ask this in Jesus' name. Amen.*

Troy Peterson, Missouri

IT'S ONLY TEMPORARY!
Scripture Reading: 1 John 2:15-17

I once had a hunting buddy comment, "Deer hunting is all I live for." Many of us have felt this way at times, and it's difficult for those most passionate about hunting to see some of the changes that have taken place over the years.

In the early 70s there was no problem finding locations to hunt. Our neighbors hunted our land, and we hunted theirs. We didn't assign numbers to nice bucks—we knew nothing of 150 or 160 class animals. There were no trophy hunters in the bunch because any deer was a trophy by our standards. Many deer hunters are now calling it quits because they can't locate a woodlot on which to hunt. With the ever increasing movement of urbanites to the country, we no longer know some of our neighbors although we're aware they don't want hunters on their property. With the growth of trophy management, access to some of the better deer woods has become an expensive proposition. And, as of this writing, Chronic Wasting Disease—the nemesis of western deer herds—has been discovered in my home state of Wisconsin. Drastic corrective measures are taking place; and if the disease spreads, deer and deer hunting throughout the region could suffer tremendously.

As Christians, we realize the things of this world are temporal, and the joy we find in these things can be short-lived. The Bible instructs that each one of us will eventually have to face God and give an account of our lives on earth. Any trophies we have accumulated here will be of no consequence there. Certainly, deer hunting can be a blessing. The fellowship with friends and family, and the interaction with God's creation are cause for thanks and praise. But is deer hunting "all we live for"? We should follow the words of Paul when he said, ". . . I consider everything a loss compared to the surpassing greatness of knowing Christ Jesus my Lord" (Philippians 3:8a). And again, "For to me, to live is Christ and to die is gain" (Philippians 1:21). Let's live for the Lord!

Prayer: *Lord, help me to always put You first. Help me to always remember that ". . . what is seen is temporary, but what is unseen is eternal" (2 Corinthians 4:18). In Jesus' name. Amen.*

Gregg Wheeler, Wisconsin

THE WRESTLING MATCH
Scripture Reading: Romans 6:11-14

After a poor shot and a long chase, I found myself in a wrestling match with a deer. I thought then, as I do now, when thinking about that day, how we are often either wrestling with God or various kinds of evil.

We often come from sinful backgrounds and wrestle with things like smoking, drinking, sexual immorality, lying, stealing, and cheating—just to name a few. Not necessarily the acts themselves, but the thoughts and motives behind them are frequently what we struggle with the most.

However, with Jesus as our Lord and Savior, God has promised to not give us more than we can handle; and He always gives us a way out. The Bible declares, "No temptation has seized you except what is common to man. And God is faithful; he will not let you be tempted beyond what you can bear. But when you are tempted, he will also provide a way out so that you can stand up under it" (1 Corinthians 10:13). There is always at least a split second before you do something you know is wrong that you can utilize one of God's greatest gifts—free will.

Prayer: *Heavenly Father, thank You for the gifts of Your Son Jesus Christ, for our salvation, and for the freedom to choose Your will over ours. Help us to willfully rely on You to get us through these struggles. In Jesus' name we pray. Amen.*

Monty Klatt, Minnesota

Devotions for Deer Hunters

THE OLD RIFLE
Scripture Reading: Romans 10:9-13

Among my most prized possessions is a well-used Model 722 Remington .300 Savage. I like to shoot the old gun and hunt with it not because it is the most accurate, most attractive, most powerful, or best-balanced rifle I own—but because of the memories that it brings to me.

The gun was purchased by my father-in-law shortly after Remington brought out this model in 1948. He liked the rifle very much and used it to take many fine bucks. I was privileged to share many of those hunts with him, and many others I learned about from stories told by him and by others.

So the old gun reminds me of many pleasant hunts, but it also reminds me of my shortness of life. It seems like only yesterday that my father-in-law was strong and healthy, always insisting that he take the roughest and thickest part of the deer drive because he thought that someone else might skirt around these difficult places where the big bucks often hid. He went to be with the Lord fifteen years ago, the result of a massive heart attack.

My father-in-law was a faithful Christian, and I know he was prepared to die. What about you? If this should be your day to die, are you ready? If not, put your faith in Jesus Christ today. Tomorrow may be too late!

Prayer: *Lord, help me to live this day as if it were my last. Forgive me of my sins and save my soul through faith in Jesus Christ my Lord. Amen.*

John V. Miller, Jr., West Virginia

COVERING YOUR BLIND SIDE
Scripture Reading: Matthew 4:1-11

My wife, who is an avid deer hunter, recently observed, "You cannot watch 360 degrees from a deer stand." I agreed that watching in all directions is difficult, but it is often necessary because some of the best stands are in general crossing areas where a deer may come from almost any direction. Most of us can tell some tales about deer that came in from our "blind side."

Over the years I have learned a few things that can help a hunter cover a wide area. For example: (1) Some kind of swivel seat is often helpful. (2) Standing allows the hunter to swivel his body and pivot his feet. (3) An enclosed blind that will cover a hunter's movement will allow an individual to see in all directions.

In a somewhat similar fashion, our adversary, the devil, is always trying to sneak in on our blind side and tempt us to sin. Here are some tips to hold up under temptation. (1) Flee temptation, 2 Timothy 2:22. At the first hint of a tempting situation, get away to a safer environment. (2) Pray for strength to resist temptation. (3) Ask another Christian to pray with you. (4) Memorize Bible verses to think about when you are being tempted.

Keep alert! Remember, the devil is always out there sneaking up on our "blind side."

Prayer: *Our Father, forgive me of my sins. Make me alert to the temptations of the devil and give me strength to resist.*

John V. Miller, Jr., West Virginia

THE RIGHT TRAIL
Scripture Reading: Psalm 27:7-14

A young hunter I know once hunted deer on a farm in our county. He never took the time to effectively scout the area, nor did he know what to look for in the way of field sign. Deer season found the man hunting diligently over some unbelievable trails for several days. He picked a timbered area near a pond and had set up on a trail that was just littered with cloven hoof prints.

This place seemed just right to him until the sun rose, and hours later he found out he wasn't on a deer trail at all. It turns out, had he been hunting Nubian goats, he would have been in a real hot spot!

The Bible tells us that, "There is a way that seems right to a man, but in the end it leads to death" (Proverbs 14:12). Just because the trail you are on is well-traveled doesn't mean you are on the right one.

The Bible reveals that the path to destruction is well-worn, but the path to righteousness is seldom found. The right path leads to our Heavenly Father. Are you on that path or are you on another? Right now you are on a road, and every sunset finds you a little closer to its end. Ask Christ to come into your heart today and take control of your life and to forgive you of your sins. Make a choice to walk down His path!

Prayer: *Dear Lord, I know that Your word is the lamp that lights my path. Thanks for sending Your Son to show us the way home. Amen.*

Troy Peterson, Missouri

THE HAND THAT FEEDS YOU
Scripture Reading: Matthew 6:26

Take a moment to observe the daily lives of the woodland animals. Most are incapable of providing for their next meal, and yet their survival depends on it. Can you imagine how worried you would be if you had no control over the next meal?

God has planned for the needs of every animal from the smallest to the largest. The oak trees not only provide a shelter, but also a dinner table. God has provided a wide variety of foods for all the creatures. They are not forgotten.

We humans are normally so used to knowing where our next meal comes from that we often take it for granted. Let's not forget the hand that not only feeds the animals, but us as well.

Prayer: *Lord, thanks for providing our daily needs, especially the food we will have today.*

Troy Peterson, Missouri

THE PERFECT STAND
Scripture Reading: Psalm 127

I don't know how I do it, but I can select some of the best deer stand locations. You know, those places that seem just perfect: terrain funnels with good browse and just the right sized tree at just the right angle for both shooting and keeping down wind. As I sit there, I am so sure of myself; I'm already planning my evening of skinning and dressing. The only problem is, most of the time no deer ever appear. It's as if they don't know about this wonderful spot yet. So, I sit there befuddled and discouraged.

Sometimes I do nearly the same thing as a Christian. I come up with a good idea, one that I am certain God would be pleased with; and I pursue it. Everything seems perfect except the results. Often it falls flat. How could such a well-intentioned plan fail? Perhaps I was trying to do something for God without first seeking His thoughts and power. I guess it is an old problem because Solomon wrote about the same thing in Psalm 127, "Unless the LORD builds the house, its builders labor in vain. Unless the LORD watches over the city, the watchmen stand guard in vain" (v. 1). God's will and his power are far more important than my plans and efforts. On the other hand, nothing can stop me when I am doing what God wants, in His strength, even if it doesn't seem like the perfect set-up to me.

Prayer: *Heavenly Father, unless I follow Your plan and rely on Your power, it ends up a mess. Help me to see what You are doing, so I can join in. I ask this in Jesus' name. Amen.*

Leonard Rex, North Carolina

THE ULTIMATE GUIDE
Scripture Reading: Proverbs 3:5-6

Have you ever traveled countless miles to hunt, only to find out that it was nothing like you expected it to be? The terrain was too rugged, the area too vast, and all the wildlife seemed to have migrated to another country. That is why many people hire a guide—someone who knows the animal's habits, is familiar with the territory, and can keep you from getting lost. Hiring a good, reliable guide is usually money and time well spent. Maybe you yourself have used a guide in the past that you would recommend very highly.

We have just such a Guide in this life—His name is Jesus. I highly recommend Him when hunting for things such as truth, meaning, acceptance, and forgiveness. John sixteen says that the Holy Spirit guides us into truth, "But when he, the Spirit of truth, comes, he will guide you into all truth" (v. 13a).

The Lord sees the obstacles and the storms before we do. He knows where to find food for our bodies and food for our souls. At times when we can't see the path, He leads best. I have been in the wilderness in an unfamiliar place as nightfall approached. It sure was a good feeling to know someone knew the way out!

Prayer: *Lord, I have tried to forge my own trail in life, and I have failed. Please be my Guide and lead me in a right path.*

Troy Peterson, Missouri

Devotions for Deer Hunters

LOST
Scripture Reading: John 3:10-18

Twice I have become lost while scouting for deer. In both cases I was in country in which I had previously been, but didn't know very well. In both instances it was getting dark when I came to realize I was lost. In the first case, I had to spend the night in the woods in a cold rain; but in the second I was eventually able to find my way back to the road where my vehicle was parked.

What was the difference between these two experiences? In the second experience, I had with me a compass that faithfully pointed me in the right direction. Now I try to never go in the woods without one!

Initially, the compass did not seem to be leading me in the right direction. However, I had to quit trying to navigate by my faulty sense of direction and trust the compass.

The fact is, in the great hunt for meaning and purpose in life, we are all lost and on our way to the hell that we deserve. Nevertheless, Jesus Christ will faithfully point us in the direction of abundant life if we will follow him. Just as I had to give up trying to find my way based on which direction I thought was correct and trust in the leading of the compass, we must give up trying to do it on our own and trust in Him. He is "the way and the truth and the life" (John 14:6). And again, "Salvation is found in no one else" (Acts 4:12).

Prayer: *I know I have wandered in sin. Forgive me, and may I follow Jesus Christ, the only source of salvation. Amen.*

John V. Miller, Jr., West Virginia

PRACTICE AND PRESSURE
Scripture Reading: 1 Peter 1:13-20

It's a beginner's mistake, but it can happen to anyone. What I am referring to is missing a shot because you forgot to take off the safety. How many deer (not to mention squirrels, rabbits, and birds) are still alive because someone squeezed an immobile trigger till they disappeared? Probably at least one per hunter. I know I have inadvertently given game a reprieve through my forgetfulness. Gun writers say that we train our muscles and our mind to perform the shooting operation through repeated practice. It is not a difficult set of actions: shoulder the gun, get a sight picture, snap off the safety, and squeeze the trigger. But unless the sequence becomes nearly automatic through repetition, the excitement caused by a big buck can undo our composure.

The same thing can happen when big trouble steps out of nowhere. But instead of forgetting to click off the safety, we forget to pray. It is not that we really forget prayer. We know how important it is. It is just that we may not have trained ourselves to talk with God as part of an automatic response. How do we do that? We prepare ourselves for crises by our everyday devotional times. When I talk with God each morning about my needs and the needs of others, my mind and my heart are ready to respond with prayer whenever the pressure peaks. Let's take the advice of someone who learned this the hard way: "The end of all things is near. Therefore be clear minded and self-controlled so that you can pray" (1 Peter 4:7, NIV).

Prayer: *Lord Jesus, by the daily discipline of talking with You, make me ready to respond with faith and prayer when the pressure is on.*

Leonard Rex, North Carolina

Devotions for Deer Hunters

BE READY
Scripture Reading: Matthew 24:36-44

I had selected a stand site on a bench on the end of a long ridge. Trails crossed the bench and also ran up and down the ridge. It was difficult to see all these trails from one location so I studied the area and carefully selected what seemed to be the best spot from which to watch. I watched all day without seeing a deer; but the spot was so promising, I stayed on my post.

Late in the afternoon; a flicker of movement on my left caught my attention and I quickly turned my head to see what was moving. That was a big mistake! Immediately I heard a piercing snort that was followed by the sight of numerous white tails flashing through the trees.

With all my careful planning and patience, I was not prepared when the critical moment arrived. I should have disciplined myself to make every movement (especially of my head and hands) very slowly, or I should have built a ground blind to hide my movements.

Most deer hunters have a few stories like that to tell. Although they thought they were ready, when the moment of truth arrived they were not; and it cost them a trophy.

In the great hunt of life, many are not prepared. They know that they will eventually meet Jesus Christ through death or the second coming and face judgment. They think they are ready because they belong to a church, or they have done lots of "good things" and not many "bad things." The Bible makes it clear that our good deeds will not save us from the punishment that we deserve because of our sin. It is only by accepting Jesus Christ as Savior and Lord that we can be saved. Won't you come to him today so you will be fully prepared?

Prayer: *Lord, I want to be prepared to meet You. Thank You for sending the Lord Jesus to pay the price for* our sin. Come into my heart and life today. In Your name I pray. Amen.

John V. Miller, Jr., West Virginia

GOD'S FAN
Scripture Reading: Psalm 46:8-11

It was still dark when I made it down to the river's edge to paddle across the Niobrara River in northern Nebraska. The air was warmer than normal for mid-November, and the wind was brisk. So brisk that I had a hard time keeping the canoe under control for the short float across the river. I love a challenge, but paddling in the dark had me praying out loud until I reached the opposite shore.

After pulling the canoe into tall marsh grass, I swung my backpack and rifle over my shoulder for the uphill climb ahead. I dressed very light that morning, knowing I had to climb up out of the river valley to my stand at the end of the long draw. But this was like t-shirt weather compared to other years. I had practiced this climb in my mind many a day while working out on my aerobic stair climber in my basement—stopping every sixty yards or so to suck some more air and let my heart rate slow a little.

Well that's how I started each day of my four day hunt on a ranch in Nebraska. I had sat long days in my tree stand overlooking the huge draw to my left and the sand hills in front of me. The wind was relentless—up and down, gusts and gentle breezes coming out of the draw. At times the tree swayed so much that I wondered if I'd be able to hold on a buck if one did appear!

On the third day, I took a walk out into the sandhills to get a different perspective on the ranch. Miles of rolling grassy hills. I walked away from the river for about one hour and then swung back towards the river to finish my day in the tree. As I walked over what appeared to be one of the last big sandy hills, I got a glimpse of a deer. I shouldered my .243 and peered thru the scope—nice buck, tall rack, swayed belly. The problem was he was just swinging away from me at about 250 yards and heading for the tree line. You know the drill now, "Lord help me!" That's when I realized where I was. I'm watching that buck walk right under my tree stand and disappear down into the draw! Why?! After all that time sitting up there and seeing nothing, I take a little walk and MR. BUCK walks below my stand!

The fourth and final day I was determined to sit there to last light regardless of what was out there. Same drill as before, sun comes up, and the temperature rises, and the wind starts blowing. My face is red from wind burn and my lips are dry and cracked. But, "I'm staying put today!"

By noon I'm talking to God and making deals and promising change if he shows that or any other buck today. "Let's make a deal, Lord. You bless me and I'll be a better husband, father, employee or I'll put another ten dollars in the plate next week!"

Now it's counting down time to last light, you know—the best time for huge bucks to be roaming for their girlfriends. The wind hasn't slowed, and the light is almost gone when out of nowhere comes an experience that will be with me until I die. The wind stops blowing like someone simply turned the blower off! That's when I heard what I had been missing those past four days—silence, nothing moving. That's when the quiet voice came into the ear of my heart and said, "BE STILL AND KNOW THAT I AM GOD!" My eyes flooded with tears and ran down onto my mustache and lips. Never before had a deer hunt ended with such peace and joy. I knew that my God had provided the experience and the hope for another season.

Prayer: *Lord, thank You for reminding us that You are in complete control. Help me to always keep You in first place. I ask this in Jesus' name. Amen.*

Tom Draper, Wisconsin

Devotions for Deer Hunters

TREES!
Scripture Reading: Luke 4:46-49

A week before the opening of the gun deer season in 1998, there was a significant wind storm in our area. The winds reached sixty-five miles per hour for several hours.

On opening day I picked my way through fallen branches and trees to find my tree stand still intact. As the sun came up, I couldn't believe how different the woods that I knew so well looked.

As I gazed around that morning, it struck me that there were some very large trees that were blown over while just a few feet away a much smaller tree remained standing. A big tree that was much older than me was pulled up by its roots while a sapling just a few years old stood just as tall as it did a week before.

There was one tree that must have been sixty-five feet tall with a diameter of fifteen feet that was blown down. On the outside the tree looked like the picture of health; but when the tree came down, I could see that the inside was completely rotten.

Another very tall cedar tree was laying on its side with its roots sticking in the air. The problem with this tree was that the roots could not grasp anything solid.

Before the next storm comes, ask yourself: Is there anything in my life that is rotten? Are my "roots" grasping something solid?

Prayer: *Lord God, point out any sins in my life and forgive me as I confess them now. Help me "lay my foundation on solid rock." I ask these things in Christ's name. Amen.*

Jim Molter, Wisconsin

MY FIRST DEER
Scripture Reading: Luke 11:1-13

My head bowed, eyes shut, and my hands clasped together, I prayed aloud in my Sunday School class, "Please, God, help me or my dad get a deer this next weekend." Would God answer my prayer?

From my tree stand, I could see most of the meadow. It was covered in swamp grass-like vegetation. In my lap I rested the twenty-gauge slug gun. This was the weekend I had prayed for the week before.

Dad and I had hurried to this spot. After setting my stand up, Dad had left me to go to his own stand. Suddenly, I heard something scurrying on the bark. I looked down and saw a tiny mouse dash from one hole in the tree limb to another hole. I struggled to keep myself from letting out a scream. A few minutes after opening time, I heard yet another rustle. However, when I looked down at the limb in front of me, there was no mouse running across it. I looked at the field in front of me. Cautiously grazing was a deer. I could not see a rack so I assumed it was a doe. I pulled my weapon to my shoulder, looked down the barrel to focus the sight on the animal, and slowly squeezed the trigger.

After the shot, I pulled the gun down and reloaded it. I looked at where the deer had been standing. There was nothing there; yet the grass was so high that even if a deer had fallen there, I wouldn't be able to see it. There was nobody, yet I didn't hear or see anything running away. I worried to myself, "Did I miss it?"

After about three minutes, I remembered to blow my grunt call just like my dad had told me if I got one. My father heard the grunt and was so excited that he brought his longbow yet forgot his quiver! In Minnesota you can bow hunt during the deer gun season.

When he came, he asked me, "Did you get one?"

"I don't know," I replied. "Is there one there?" I

pointed my hand in the direction of where the deer had been.

Dad looked at a different area, and then said, "Nope."

"No," I once again pointed at the spot. "Over there."

He walked over to inspect the spot. A smile lit up his face, "Yep, Abbie. You got him in the neck!" Him? I thought to myself. Isn't it a doe? He finished, "You got a button buck."

I later saw my deer. He had polished buttons, yet was an adult buck. His antlers had either not fully developed or had broken off. He was the most beautiful deer I had ever seen! God had answered my prayer! Yet my prayer was so insignificant and small. God can answer your prayers, too. He may not answer them the way you want Him to, but He'll hear every word of yours, because He loves YOU!

Prayer: *Heavenly Father, thank You that there is no request too large or too small for You. Answer my prayers in the way that is best. I ask this in Jesus' name. Amen.*

Abbie Rakow, Minnesota

MY PERSONAL GUIDE
Scripture Reading: Hebrews 13:1-8

It was a calm, slightly overcast morning just as it had been numerous times in my past when I set out for a full day of hunting. It was a large, new, and unfamiliar stretch of bottom swamp land near The Lower Suwannee River Unit in my home state of Florida. I had hunted with my dad since I was eight years old; and now in my late thirties, I had the confidence and experience of using a compass—my personal guide. My compass would help me navigate through any areas exempt from humans.

Today I would be using the still-hunt, spot, and stalk approach to harvest my quarry. After many hours of moving through tangles of briars, thickets, and swamps, I sat down to have a bite to eat and slumber under an old, mossy cypress tree. I had checked my compass periodically and had the peace that all was going as planned. My guide—the compass, was with me.

After lunch and a short nap, I began my trek once again; but this time I had neglected to check my compass before starting out. Some time into my hunt, it dawned on me that I needed to check my compass for direction. That's when things dramatically changed. I had lost my compass; my guide was gone!

I then began to head in the direction that I thought was the right way out. Time was of the essence. Well, time passed; and it began to rain. It was getting dark, and I was very lost. I knew better than to panic, but I needed help drastically so I prayed to God and asked for His help. As I stood there wondering how He could help me in this situation, I happened to look down and saw something in the leaves. When I picked it up, it was a compass that another hunter had evidently dropped in the past! It was a miracle! Someone I didn't know had helped save me!

In John 3:16 the Bible states, "For God so loved the

world that he gave his one and only Son, that whoever believes in him shall not perish but have eternal life." If you have become lost in life's struggles, when everything seems to be raining down on you and life looks hopelessly dark, just ask God for help. He has given us a guide—our compass—Jesus. God's Son Jesus died on the cross so that we might be saved. In Hebrews 13:5 God has said, "Never will I leave you; never will I forsake you." Jesus will always be there to help us. No matter where we go or what we do, He will always be there. He has proved it to me time and again. Why not try Him and see?

Prayer: *Thank You, Lord, for caring about the details of my life. Thank You for being my constant guide. Direct me in the way You want me to go. In Jesus' name. Amen.*

Rev. Ed Dedmon, Wisconsin

INNOCENT OR GUILTY?
Scripture Reading: Romans 13:1-8

During the 2000 Minnesota firearms deer hunting season, I was invited by a friend to hunt deer with him on a private farm. When it came time to purchase my license, I had doubts of which section of hunting zone this farm was in so I asked the clerk to confirm with the Department of Natural Resources which was the proper hunting section. Because the farm was on the line of two different hunting zones, I was advised to purchase the more expensive All State Buck Deer License. This license covered the whole state except one small section somewhere in the area where I was hunting.

With the excitement of a new hunting opportunity and meeting several relatives of my friend, I was most excited to hunt on a private farm. After the first two days of hunting, we were fortunate to get three deer for six hunters. Because I like to process my own deer, I put my license on one of the deer which someone else had shot.

We went to register the deer. The others registered their deer while I filled the car with gas. When I paid for the gas, I asked the attendant which hunting section the hunters who had just registered their deer had used. I entered that section on the deer registration tag of my license.

One tradition this group of hunters had was to go out for a BIG breakfast before heading home as a way of celebrating the hunt. While discussing the hunt I asked, "Which section did you use to register your deer?" I had entered the wrong section of the hunting zone. But, because there was a shortage of license regulations, we concluded this was probably a small issue—and after all the deer was registered.

While on a business trip about a month later, my wife said a game warden had called and said he would call back. I thought he was going to verify where the deer was shot and correct my error.

At the end of a very bad day at work, we finally connected. He first confirmed I had registered the deer in the wrong section, and I confessed to an honest mistake.

He then asked who had shot the deer. Again, I was honest and said one of my friends. I was then informed that I had broken the law. When a person purchases the more expensive license it is illegal to party hunt (which means you must shoot the deer, no one else can fill this tag). Because it was an honest mistake, he said that if I informed him of the farm I was hunting on and all the others with whom I was hunting, he would drop one offense; and I could pay a small fine. When I said I would not turn in my friends, he threatened me with several hundred dollars in fines, thirty days in jail, no hunting or fishing privileges for ten years and the confiscation of my new truck! He then asked if I would reconsider. I said "NO!"

Later I appeared in court armed only with the title of my truck and a good book. I faced the judge. When he asked, "Innocent or guilty?" I stated that I respected the court and had made a couple of innocent mistakes. I pleaded guilty and asked for a fair verdict. I waived the right to an attorney trusting in the judge's decision.

The judge then asked me to explain the circumstances, and I did. The judge then asked the game warden his view and determination what to do. He stated that ignorance of the law is not an excuse. He also stated that I should have checked with the Department of Natural Resources website to determine where I had hunted. Furthermore, the small print on the back of my turned in deer registration license said not to party hunt.

I was fined $350.00, given one year probation and lost my hunting privileges for three years. I felt relieved to be driving home in my truck. I concluded that we cannot use ignorance to break the law, and we are all accountable to the authority that is placed over us. Romans 13:1a states, "Everyone must submit himself to the governing authorities, for there is no authority except that which God has established."

Prayer: *Lord God, help me to be the citizen You want me to be. I ask this in Jesus' name. Amen.*

Rick Morical, Minnesota

THE UNIVERSAL HUNT
Scripture Reading: John 3:1-21

Generally, when talking about hunting, we focus on the getting to, finding, and shooting of game. But what about "the hunt" that every person focuses on at one point or another in his life?

It seems that almost everyday in some way we hunt. We hunt for self-gratification, life's meaning, or perhaps a long list of material things.

We were created to have companionship with God. It was God who breathed into the first human the breath of life and linked us to Himself (see Genesis 2:7).

Ever since the fall of humanity into the pit of sin (Genesis 3), our souls have longed for companionship with our Creator. So, we spend our days hunting, not knowing for what we are hunting or even where to look. We are really trying to fill a void in our lives. A void that only Jesus Christ can fill.

In John 3 Jesus talked about being born again. He explained how we can have companionship with God. When we accept what Jesus did for each and every one of us by dying on the cross to take away the sins of the world, the hunt is finally over. Praise the Lord!

Prayer: *Thank You, Jesus, for dying for us so we can live with You forever. Amen.*

Monty Klatt, Minnesota

FUNDAMENTALS
Scripture Reading: Colossians 3:1-10

My wife is the most efficient deer hunter I know. By that I mean she has bagged more deer for the amount of time actually spent hunting. She seldom fails to have a buck before noon on opening day. The boom of her old .270 nearly always means a deer to drag.

Yet she is not an outstanding marksmen, never has read a book or magazine article on deer hunting, doesn't know the stages of the rut and can't blow a grunt call or identify how to use deer scents.

How is she so successful? She concentrates on the fundamentals, and she does these very well. She usually hunts from a tree stand in an excellent location. She has learned to sit very still; and when she must move, she does so very slowly. She is patient and does not pull the trigger until she has a sure shot. Her rifle is always sighted in properly, and she practices with it before season opens.

Life is a lot like deer hunting—there are certain fundamentals that we must master if we are to be successful. First, we must realize that we are hopelessly lost in sin (Romans 3:23) and must trust Jesus Christ to save us (Acts 2:38). Unless we trust Jesus to save us, we are lost and on our way to hell (Romans 6:23).

Second, we must read the Bible. In it we can find strength, guidance, and inspiration for life (Psalm 119:9). Finally, we must worship God in a Christian fellowship. Christians strengthen and support each other (Hebrews 10:25).

There are many things we can do to make ourselves better deer hunters and more dynamic Christians, but the fundamentals are essential. Are your practicing the fundamentals?

Prayer: *Dear God help me today to concentrate on*

those things that are most important, the things of Your kingdom and righteousness. Give me the faith to trust in You. In Christ's name. Amen.

John V. Miller, Jr., West Virginia

MY CHOICE, TO BE AN EXAMPLE
Scripture Reading: Titus 2:6-8

It had just finished raining, and the wind was blowing a cold front (for Florida) into Gulf Hammock. Nothing was moving; it was the last weekend of hunting season, January, 1966, with nothing harvested. I was in a sad mood. My son Eddie was eleven years old and had been hunting with me for three years; he was at my side as we tried to push a deer out of the thickets. In those days wild hogs could only be harvested during the first nine days of the season in November; but in my desire for game, I had decided to shoot one anyway because the check station was locked up tight and no one else was in the woods. Who would know?

As we approached a downed tree, a wild pig ran out of the tree top—perfect for my shotgun. At that point several things happened: I raised the shotgun, pushed the safety off, found the pig with my bead, thought about my son standing next to me, thought about my wife and daughter at home, and thought about what God would think of me . . . I could not pull the trigger. I lowered the gun and explained to Eddie that it would not be right to shoot the pig because they were not in season.

On the way out of the management land, we passed the locked check station; and around the next turn the narrow dirt road was blocked by two game management vehicles. Our truck, trailer, and the jeep on the trailer were searched. Not finding any illegal game, they wished us a good day; and we drove home.

All the way home, I thanked God for reminding me to do the right thing and to be a good example for my son who is now an ordained minister in Wisconsin. We still enjoy hunting together and rehashing the good old memories.

Prayer: *Lord, thank You for reminding us that You see,* *hear, and know everything. Give me a heart to obey You at all times. I ask this in Jesus' name. Amen.*

Ed Dedmon (Senior), Florida

NO COINCIDENCE
Scripture Reading: Matthew 21:18-22

The opening day of Wisconsin's gun deer season is a tradition I will always cherish fondly. Ten years of ineffaceable hunting memories were cast with my father amidst the wonders and splendor of the forest. To posture for Nimrod's success in 1998, I had previously scouted deer sign, built a ground stand above a dense swamp with good visibility, and sighted in my .308 Savage. I was feeling especially optimistic about the upcoming hunt. It would prove a glorious season.

Saturday morning, November twenty-first, began with enthusiastic prayer. Dress, eat, and pack defined my zero-dark-early ritual before the sixteen mile rendezvous with the other hunters from our remaining party. "The best laid plans of mice and men," I arrived eagerly to my stand in quiet exhilaration. Now listen and wait patiently! The chill of the early morning air gave way to a welcoming sun. At 7:45 a.m., a faint disturbance portended venison on the hoof.

The doe was bounding eastward along the swamp's edge, but raising my rifle for a better look espied instead a jaw-dropping, muscular-bodied, mature eight-pointer positioned precisely in my crosshairs. That buck could have easily veered any direction on the compass. In utter disbelief, the biggest buck to ever grace my scope was staring at me thirty-five yards away. A second later, the smooth pull of my trigger manifested a resounding echo through the forest. I couldn't believe it when he abruptly swung north into dense alders seemingly unaffected. Regaining my composure, I searched in vain for HBT; hair, blood, and tracks. Half hour of tracking returned me to my stand, heart in stomach. I thanked the Lord aloud, albeit disappointed, for providing the opportunity to at least view the magnificent animal.

Two hours of miserable "what ifs" followed. Could I

have indeed missed? Three hunters suddenly appeared on a drive, one of them stopping briefly to chat. I shared with him my futility. . .gall and wormwood still in my throat. He rejoined his party a slow stalk later, but soon returned with some curious investigative-type questions (i.e., Where did I aim on him?, etc.) After the "interrogation," or confirmation, we walked nearly 80 yards together into the swamp tangle toward the other two hunters in his group. One of them had spotted an anomaly from off the adjacent logging road, which happened to be my beautiful buck concealed tightly in thick brush. It would have required Superman's vision to even remotely recognize the outline of a Whitetail, unless divinely inspired. For a moment, I was certain they were angels. The hunters shared their testimony explaining to me that before accepting the Lord one year earlier they would have claimed the buck by rights. Rather, I was instructed to mount him above my own fireplace for posterity. They also provided me with a small pocket Bible. We parted company one in spirit, as I attended to the deer. I was additionally blessed with the help of a hunter using his ATV.

A mini drama unfolded that day. Anticipation, failure, redemption, victory. Despite my self-doubt, the Lord intended that buck for me all along. We don't have a fireplace, but the buck on my young son's wall serves as a powerful reminder of the Lord's faithfulness, and inconceivable blessings. When the Lord decides to bless you, nothing will impede His will. As hunters, always trust your rifle, be relentless in your tracking efforts, employ ethics, and remember "that in all things God works for the good of those who love Him, who have been called according to His purpose" (Romans 8:28). May God keep you safe in the woods, and reward your hunting traditions with lasting sustenance.

Prayer: *"This is the confidence we have in approaching*

God: that if we ask anything according to His will, he hears us" (1 John 5:14). Lord, thank You for the ways in which You answer prayer and use Your people to help us. May I be the answer to someone's prayer. I ask this in Jesus' name. Amen.

Matthew N. Paris, Wisconsin

GOD SMILED ON ME TODAY
Scripture Reading: Philippians 4:12-13

It was a hot November day in west Tennessee, not a day that you would think much about deer hunting. The mosquitoes were out and it was about eighty degrees on a bright sunny day. But I had two hours before my thirteen-year-old daughter's basketball game and I was itching to go deer hunting.

Most people hunt for food here and with all the hunting pressure a deer rarely lives past his second birthday. Finding a Boone & Crockett trophy deer in Weakley county is like finding a needle in a haystack.

As I waited for my daughter to get home so we could shoot some free throws before the big game tonight, I couldn't help but think about deer hunting. My daughter arrived home after what she called a hard day and said she just wanted to rest this afternoon and for me to go on deer hunting.

I had joined a deer hunting club with some of my buddies, and this would be my first time to hunt this new property. I picked up my son's muzzleloader and got my mosquito spray. The property was only ten minutes from the house. I thought this could be as much of a scouting trip as a hunting trip since I knew nothing about the farm I was about to hunt. I am a handicapped hunter and if it wasn't for my trusty Honda four-wheeler getting me to and from the field I would have had to give up hunting twenty-five years ago when I had a massive stroke. I was very blessed that over time I regained almost everything except the use of my legs. I can now get around with the use of a cane. But through the help of my family and friends and the grace of God, I haven't missed a beat in my love for hunting and fishing.

As I got to the field I grabbed my muzzleloader, my fanny pack, my doe-in-estrous scent, and my grunt call. It was 4:00 p.m. and I had an hour-and-a-half to hunt. I always carry a drag rag doused with doe-in-rut scent behind my four-wheeler to help cover my scent and also to attract bucks. I could see a nice big tree stand of one of my friends from the road. I thought it might be a good spot as it was overlooking a bean field in the river bottom. I rode my four-wheeler dragging my drag rag along the edge of the bean field and parked in the bushes behind the deer stand.

I tried my best to get up in the stand but it just wasn't going to happen as I almost fell out trying to get situated. So, I climbed down and fixed me a comfortable spot under the deer stand and leaned my muzzleloader against the first step of the ladder. As I peered through the ladder I could see the cars and trucks going by quite often down the highway.

The thought ran through my mind that I was just wasting my time, but I told myself to enjoy being out in the woods and to sit until dark. I've always thought the best way to deer hunt was just to be quiet and sit still and let the deer come to you. An hour went by and all I'd seen were two squirrels. With no deer activity I decided it couldn't hurt anything to try my old grunt call. I could still smell the scent of doe-in-estrous scent on my fingertips. I'm not a professional grunter by any means, but I grunted a few short grunts.

What happened next left me in disbelief as in my forty years of hunting I've never seen anything like it. This monster buck bolted from a thicket looking for a fight, or to protect his territory. He was heading right to me across the open bean field. It happened so quickly that when the buck stopped he was at seventy-five yards, but I hadn't even had time to get my gun ready.

I have a scope on my muzzleloader, but it didn't take any kind of optics to tell this boy was a shooter. I managed to get my gun up and get my sights on him, but he started walking again looking for the other buck. His hair was all bristled and his ears laid back as though he was ready to fight. When he stopped at sixty yards I pulled the trigger and I couldn't see a thing for a couple seconds.

When the smoke cleared, all I could see was antlers, big antlers like I've never seen before. I waited ten minutes to be sure he wasn't going to run off and that was the longest ten minutes of my life. At 5:10 I got on my four-wheeler and rode up to him. He had thirteen points and some of the longest tines that I've ever seen. He had mule deer forks on both sides and drop tines on both sides. The deer had a twenty-two-inch spread and weighed 175 pounds. It was the nicest deer that I've ever seen in my lifetime.

I've never been a big believer in using a grunt call, but after this hunt I will never ever be caught without it again. There's no doubt that the combination of my deer scent and a grunt call did the trick on this old buck. Looking back, I almost didn't go deer hunting that particular day. Had my daughter wanted to shoot basketball, then I would never have gone deer hunting. Also, I had those thoughts of "it's just too hot and the deer won't be moving." Then, after I did go hunting I almost talked myself into leaving early. The bottom line is if you get a chance to go deer hunting, you better go—you never know what's going to happen. I have hunted for forty years and spent thousands of hours in the field, but you just never know when it's going to happen. It's kind of like that old saying: "A bad day of hunting is still better than a good day at work." Just when I think life can't get any better God lets something else unbelievable happen to me. Thank You, God.

Prayer: *Lord, help me to be ready for Your blessings. Thank You that, "I can do everything through him who gives me strength" (Philippians 4:13). Amen.*

Larry Porter, Tennessee

ONCE IN A LIFETIME MOOSE HUNT (Part 1)
Scripture Reading: Proverbs 16:33

It was the culmination of a ten year dream. For nine long years I had faithfully applied for the Minnesota moose lottery. This is a drawing for a once-in-a-lifetime chance for residents to take any moose (bull, cow, or calf) by rifle or bow. Because I was not getting any younger, and the rheumatoid arthritis with which I was diagnosed was not getting any better—on the tenth year I decided to apply for a different zone. I hoped this would increase my chances of being drawn.

This new zone I applied for was entirely in the Boundary Waters Canoe Area. It had been recently formed when the Department of Natural Resources took the remotest areas of three other zones to make another new one. This meant no motors, wheels, or helpful devices for getting into the area, or for packing out a moose. Travel would be by canoe and on foot. Unlike the area for which I had previously been putting in—I knew nothing about this zone.

I was pleasantly surprised and extremely excited when notification that I had finally been drawn arrived in the mail. The church I pastor, Grace Bible Church, rejoiced with me and started praying for success. When my friend Jim Suttinger from Ohio found out that I had been drawn for a moose he made and sent me a dozen of the most beautiful wooden arrows I have ever seen. He weighted them especially for moose and then inscribed a Bible reference on each arrow. One of the references was Proverbs 12:27, "The lazy man does not roast his game, but the diligent man prizes his possessions."

Meanwhile I was shooting arrows, watching moose hunting videos, practicing calls, and learning all that I could in preparation for my once-in-a-lifetime hunt. Although I would haul a rifle along on the trip—my ultimate goal was to take a bull moose with a longbow.

I did a couple of scouting trips to the zone and found a cow moose skull, and the fairly fresh remains of a moose calf which had evidently been killed by wolves. However, I found no fresh moose tracks or droppings on either of the scouting trips which caused me concern.

The season arrived and I headed into the wilderness. A day later I was joined by my friends Art Sakaye, Tim Redingtom, and a new fellow by the name of Matt Witt. They all took time off work and at their own expense purchased provisions for the trip. Furthermore, they were committed to spending as much time as it took for me to take down a moose. According to Minnesota law they could not assist me in the actual hunt, but when I had harvested my big bull moose, Art, Tim, and Matt would help pack him out of the wilderness. They all had such a wonderful servant attitude even when the weather was less than pleasant. It either rained or snowed almost every day—and yet they kept a warm fire going, loaned me their own dry clothing, and cooked excellent meals every night.

We kept moving further back into the wilderness. Although we left some of the gear behind, we still had big loads to carry over difficult portages going from lake to lake. We had great talks and long theological discussions about the Bible, and each night they patiently put up with my preaching.

They joked that they were going to convert me back to drinking. And although I was never tempted to drink, I must admit experiencing some of the greatest times of supernatural depression and spiritual warfare I have ever faced. This didn't happen in camp—only when I was out hunting. When I returned to the camp, the depression and suicidal thoughts would fade. In fact, in camp I felt empowered by God. This was strange because for me being alone in the woods is normally a wonderful and relaxing experience. I still can't explain this except to say that it was supernatural and that the powers of darkness were certainly present—even in the wilderness. It may be they merely wanted to stop the spiritual discussions we were having from taking place. Whatever the case, it continued on through the rest of that week. It was terrible. In fact, it kept getting more and more difficult to go out to hunt and then face the spiritual onslaught I was experiencing.

The hunting was also physically draining due to the wet and cold weather. There had also been a severe blow down in that part of the Boundary Waters a couple of years earlier. There were many times when I was either walking on fallen trees or crawling under and through them.

Each day my dream of harvesting a moose continued to dwindle. The first thing that went out the window was my high hopes of taking a big bull moose with the longbow. If need be, I would take my bull with a rifle.

Next my need to take even a small bull moose disappeared. After all, a cow was legal and would taste just as good, and maybe even better!

Even though I kept striving to succeed and my friends were more than willing to continue, after a week I knew it was time to take a break. Besides, the wet and cold weather was really getting to me physically. So, we broke camp and started on the journey home empty-handed. Inside I was striving and anxious. I could feel my once-in-a-lifetime opportunity to harvest a Minnesota moose slipping helplessly through my fingers. However, as we were paddling back out I inwardly knew I would have to try again just to make sure I had given it everything I had.

Prayer: *Lord, thank You for those who encourage and help us. Thank You for friends who invest their time, treasures, and talents so that we might realize our dreams. May You make me to be a source of comfort* *and encouragement to others. I ask this in Jesus' name. Amen.*

Dr. Tom Rakow, Minnesota

ONCE IN A LIFETIME MOOSE HUNT (Part 2)
Scripture Reading: Ecclesiastes 3:1-8

A few days later I headed back into the wilderness alone. I paddled a one-person canoe and, along with my limited food and gear, had packed a rolled up inflatable raft which was large enough to transport a boned-out moose. Although a few years earlier I and a couple others had helped my friend Art Sakaye pack out his Pope and Young bull, I knew doing it all alone would pose a major problem. Whenever I started thinking about the difficulty of such a task, I reminded myself, "Packing a moose out is not a problem, but NOT having a moose to pack out IS a problem!"

I set up camp and invested the entire next day just looking for fresh moose sign. Starting out before daylight and making a fifteen mile plus hike over hills, through swamps, brush, and streams, I arrived back in camp just before dark. On the far end of my loop (about eight miles away) I had found a bull rub and at least two different sets of fresh tracks. At last there was some hope! Even so, on the inside I was still striving and concerned about blowing my once-in-a-lifetime opportunity. Time was running out.

To get near the fresh sign by canoe required a lot of paddling and about eight portages, so I opted to travel by foot. I moved camp closer, but it still took two-and-a-half hours just to walk from my new camp to the fresh moose sign. Nevertheless, I was desperate and this was the hottest place I had found to hunt.

Making the long trip back to camp the next evening I started contemplating how a smaller cow moose or a calf would be much easier to get out of this remote area. I started praying to that end. Better yet, maybe I could shoot a hollow moose! You know, something like those hollow milk chocolate bunnies stores sell at Easter time.

That night in my tent I was thinking about all the

planning, preparing, and praying that had gone into this hunt. I thought of how my wife Beth, our girls, and the church had seriously prayed for me and spoken words of encouragement. Personally I had prayed for this opportunity to hunt moose for many years. I thought of Art, Tim, and Matt and how they'd spent time and money to help me out. I thought of numerous others who had loaned me equipment and even canoes so I could make the trip. Nevertheless, now it was looking more and more hopeless. My once-in-a-lifetime opportunity to hunt moose was rapidly going down the drain. Yes, time was running out. But then something happened that put things in their proper perspective.

That night as I lay in my tent alone, I was turning the dial on my transistor radio when I picked up a Christian radio station on the skip. I only heard about three minutes, but it was exactly what I needed. It was a call-in program with Joni Erickson Tada as the guest. Joni is a quadriplegic who (despite her physical disability) has ministered powerfully to multitudes. Joni had written a book, and a male caller (perhaps someone also with a disability) had phoned to tell her, "I really appreciate what you had to say in your book. Especially where you state that there are more important things in this life than being able to walk."

Friend, I want to tell you that those few words from that caller regarding Joni's book immediately changed my perspective. Although I was in a remote part of the wilderness where no wheelchair could travel, God chose to use a quadriplegic and an unknown caller to speak to me. I thought, "Surely if there are more important things in this life than being able to walk, there are also a whole lot more important things in life than Tom Rakow harvesting a moose!" From that point on, the pressure was off and I started truly enjoying the hunt. The lakes seemed clearer, and the colorful fall leaves much brighter.

But as a wise man once said, "There is a time for

everything, and a season for every activity under heaven" (Ecclesiastes 3:1). Indeed, there is "a time to search and a time to give up" (Ecclesiastes 3:6a). On the fifth day of this second attempt I headed back home with no moose. However, I did possess a far greater appreciation for the unique opportunity I had been given to go on a "once-in-a-lifetime moose hunt."

Prayer: *Heavenly Father, thank You for speaking to us through other people. Amen.*

Dr. Tom Rakow, Minnesota

WHAT'S YOUR FAVORITE COLOR?
Scripture Reading: Psalm 1

It was October and I was resting comfortably in my tree stand. I was waiting patiently for that magical time when deer start feeding from their ridge-top bedding area to the acorn strewn valleys below. Turkeys fed their way through the undergrowth, putting softly to each other.

As I looked through the canopy of color, I thought that I should tell God which color I liked the best. As the sun reached through the many small openings, the leaves seemed to literally glow. It appeared that if the sun were to be extinguished at this moment, the trees would supply all the light needed. I smiled as I thought that leaves could glow. I refocused on picking my favorite color.

When I looked from tree to tree, I witnessed versions of yellow, orange, red, green, brown . . . what an incredible scene! Here was every blend of these colors, sometimes mixed intricately within a single leaf. Some had a type of red veining with green surrounding as if the artist wanted to highlight the middle. There were none that didn't deserve top honor.

Then I saw it. It was a maple tree that seemed to glow the brightest. The yellow to orange and then to some other indescribable glow was my favorite. I was in awe of this color and yet I could not tell God what it was. I could only say, "God, that's my favorite." Romans 1:20 tells us that there will be no excuse for not knowing there is a God. Creation has provided enough proof. He's created a universe where words don't even exist to describe the color of a leaf. That is not the result of an accident. It can only come from a Creator—God Himself.

Prayer: *O Lord, make me into something that brings great pleasure to You. In Jesus' name. Amen.*

Peter Koenig, Wisconsin

THE GRAND FINALE
Scripture Reading: Psalm 150:1-6

Driving in the darkness of predawn, the now disappearing two-lane highway had become a flawless white ribbon of virgin snow. As I neared my destination, faint oncoming headlights glimmered over a distant hill, and I noticed they began to slow at the same pace as I. As the oncoming vehicle met me, we both came to a stop, nose to nose, in the middle of the highway. The window rolled down and my hunting partner motioned for me to follow his lead as he backed his van into the deep snow that covered his driveway. I was excited to deer hunt these last two days of the archery season because the weather was perfectly cold, the northwest wind wasn't gale force for a change and evidence of deer movement was everywhere. But it was more than just that. In two short days, I would have to wait nine more months for the birth of next year's bow hunting season. Just thinking about that made me ache.

The snow continued to fall as we got our gear organized for the bitterly cold morning hunt. Wading slowly through the deep snow, we made our way to our stands, stopping every fifty yards or so to quietly whisper our plans for the morning hunt and get each other stoked before going our separate ways. I crept stealthily to my stand and slowly scaled the tree. Once settled and sitting still, I let the perfect silence of the Minnesota winter woods envelope me. This is always one of life's finest moments for me; and every time I do it, I like it more, want it more, and thank God for the privilege.

Comfortably warm in layers of cammies, my nearby bow was at the ready with a nocked arrow, hands warm in a muff and only my eyes uncovered to take it all in. God's rheostat slowly took the woods from dreamscape to dawn. Seeing deer movement eighty yards in the distance, I slowly eased my hand over to my bow, curling my fingers around the grip and executing a slow motion torque in their direction. My adrenaline pumped as I watched the gray bodies glide effortlessly through snow. Three does were making their way through heavy brush and suddenly stopped downwind of me, nosing the air. "Busted!" I thought to myself. They turned and warily nosed the air again, passing forty yards from me now—but still too far for a shot with the forty-seven pounds I pull. Ever hopeful they would clear the brush and come nearer, I locked my release on my bowstring and started to draw. At that same moment, they began the telltale walk of fear, tails straight out, heads down, and placing hooves methodically in preparation for escape. They bolted so I eased my pull and put my frozen hands back in my muff. The zero degree cold was starting to give me the shivers. By 9:00 a.m. even my isometrics couldn't keep me warm, so I descended the tree and made a push in my friend's direction as planned.

    I had decided to head back to my land to plow the driveway entrance and hunt the evening there. I struggled to get the plow on my frozen ATV, but eventually finished the plowing and prepared for the evening hunt in—surprise—my evergreen stand. The walk was challenging with snow two feet in places, and my stand had a foot of snow on it as well. Sitting eighteen feet up, nestled among the boughs of the snow-flocked conifer, I became a component of the tree with my stillness. Darkness fell and only an occasional grouse rippled the silence with its drumbeat wings.

    Leaving my stand in the dark without a flashlight, I waddled over the uneven terrain through deep and weightless snow. Almost to my truck, I stopped and just stood there, face lifted for a moment, as snow flakes softly landed on my eyelashes and melted on my cheeks. I set my ice-encrusted therma-mat down on the snowy path, knelt on it, and set my bow in the snow next to me. Head lowered, arms at my sides, I was struck by the need to talk with my Creator, just then, as if called. I prayed there and gave thanks for this land, for how it satisfies the passions of my heart and for how it recharges the batteries of my soul. Face raised now, and arms raised to Him as well, the icy evening wind felt good as it glazed my face. I smiled.

Prayer: *Lord God, thank You for the special time hunting allows me to spend with You!*

Linda K. Burch, Minnesota

Devotions for Deer Hunters

The Fragrance of the Season
by
Thelma L. Hintz, Minnesota

You dress real funky
So you look like a tree.
Then douse yourself
With a little doe pee.

The fragrance of the season
So I'm told
Makes the huge monster buck
A little more bold.

You get to the woods
Before first light
Shinny up a tree
And hang on tight.

You move slow and quiet
Causing no flight
Of the huge monster buck
Who's been waiting all night
To be shot by you
When you get him in your sight.

You sit real still
And give praises to the master.
All the while wishing
The sun would rise a little faster.

So this is deer hunting?
You've been waiting all year.
As the season drew nearer
You knew no fear.

The huge monster buck

is waiting for you.
He's getting impatient
As you set and stew.

You yawn and you stretch.
And let your chin droop.
Before you know it
You're out of the loop.

The fragrance of the season
Has brought him nigh.
The huge monster buck
Passes right on by.
As you're in the act
Of getting some shut eye!

When deer season's over
And all's said and done.
Give glory to the master
As He's the only one,
That we can always count on.

He's tried and He's true,
And He'll never forsake us,
Not me – not you.
He's our "fragrance for <u>all</u> seasons."

Devotions for Deer Hunters

The Hunt

Are you hunting for something you have not been able to find? Perhaps you have been looking in the wrong places. God has designed us in such a way that only He can fulfill our deepest needs and desires. Here is how you can come to have a personal relationship with God through His Son, Jesus Christ.

RECOGNIZE: First you must recognize that you have sinned and need a Savior. "For all have sinned and fall short of the glory of God" (Romans 3:23).

REPENT: Turn from your sin. To repent means to have a change of mind about your rebellion against God. The Bible says that God "commands all people everywhere to repent" (Acts 17:30).

RECEIVE: Receive the resurrected Jesus Christ as your personal Savior. Accept His sacrifice on the cross as the personal payment for your sin. Concerning Jesus Christ the gospel of John tells us, ". . . to all who received Him, to those who believed in His name, He gave the right to become children of God" (John 1:12).

REJOICE: If you have just received God's wonderful gift of salvation, you have something to rejoice about! The Bible tells us that there is even ". . . rejoicing in the presence of the angels of God over one sinner who repents" (Luke 15:10).

We would like to rejoice with you! If you would like more information about living the Christian life, write to us at the address below:

Christian Deer Hunters Association®
PO Box 432
Silver Lake, MN 55381
1-866-HIS-HUNT
website: christiandeerhunters.org

OUR PURPOSE

The Christian Deer Hunters Association® is a nonprofit, interdenominational organization which exists for the purpose of helping individuals to know and better understand the God of the Bible.

The Bible makes it clear that, as Creator, God has been and continues to be involved in every area of life. The apostle Paul said concerning Jesus Christ, ". . . by Him all things were created: things in heaven and on earth, visible, and invisible, whether thrones or powers or authorities; all things were created by Him and for Him. He is before all things, and in Him all things hold together" (Colossians 1:16-17).

With this in mind, the Christian Deer Hunters Association® desires to help each hunter more fully realize the Creator's presence. We believe that such an awareness of God will ultimately be beneficial to hunters and society as a whole.

OUR GOALS

The Christian Deer Hunters Association® seeks to fulfill their purpose for existence by means of:

Evangelization: Reaching others with the gospel of Christ.

Edification: Building up the body of Christ.

Education: Implanting the mind of Christ.

Entertainment: Providing enjoyable Bible-based materials in the name of Christ.

OUR OBJECTIVE

We believe it is possible and desirable that God be glorified in such common things as eating and drinking (see I Corinthians 10:31). Unfortunately, even many who have professed faith in Jesus Christ struggle when it comes to recognizing a responsibility before God in the area of hunting.

Therefore, a primary objective of the Christian Deer Hunters Association® is to reveal and encourage a Biblical World View approach to deer hunting. Some of the things that a Biblical World View will help to stimulate or encourage include:

- An ongoing surrender of one's life to the Lordship of Jesus Christ.
- A proper balance between hunting and family life.
- An awareness that deer hunting can be an excellent opportunity for sharing the gospel of Jesus Christ with others (Mark 16:15-16).
- The proper view towards those who are in authority, such as DNR officials (Romans 13:1-7).
- An ever-increasing gratitude of God's gracious provisions.
- An enhanced appreciation concerning the value and beauty of all that God has created and a recognition of our divinely granted role as stewards (Genesis 1:27-28; Psalm 8).
- Proper attitudes toward trespassing and other laws.
- The implementation of safety procedures which reflect a love for one's neighbor.
- The importance of faithful church attendance and involvement during the hunting season (Hebrews 10:25).
- Better stewardship practices when buying equipment.
- A wiser use of time spent while actually in the field hunting (e.g. Scripture reading, memorization, prayer, witnessing).

WHAT WE BELIEVE ABOUT:

GOD
God is one person. Yet, within this unity there are three persons of one essential nature, power, and eternity — the Father, the Son, and the Holy Spirit (Dt 6:4; Jn 1:12; Mt 28:19; Ac 5:3-4).

THE HOLY BIBLE
The Old and New Testaments are both verbally inspired by God and without error in the original manuscripts. The Scriptures are the standard by which all doctrine and behavior are to be ultimately discerned (Pr 30:5-6; 2 Ti 3:16-17; 2 Pe 1:21).

HUMANS
Man was initially created in the image of God, but through disobedience lost his once perfect nature and standing with God (Ge 1:26-27; 3). The entire human race, from Adam to the present, has failed to meet God's righteous standard (Ps 14:2-3; Ro 3:23). Humankind, being totally depraved, is in need of regeneration/the new birth. Regeneration is an act initiated by God the Holy Spirit and the result of God's grace (Tit 3:4-6; Jn 1:12-13; 3:3, 5-8, etc.).

SALVATION
Salvation is by grace through faith and not the result of human effort. Our salvation is in Jesus Christ and, apart from His work on the cross, there is no other means of escaping the wrath of God that all humans deserve (Eph 2:8-9; Ro 6:23; Jn 14:6; Ac 4:12; I Ti 2:5).

JESUS CHRIST AND HIS SECOND COMING
Jesus Christ is the express image of the invisible God who was conceived by the Holy Spirit and born of the Virgin Mary. He died upon a cross for the sins of the world, and whoever truly trusts in Him shall be saved for all eternity. He died, was buried, and rose again on the third day according to the Scriptures. He ascended to heaven in a glorified body where He now sits at the right hand of the Father. He will one day return and judge the world in righteousness (Heb 1:3; Jn 1:14; 1 Co 15:3-7; Ac 17:31). Jesus Christ's personal return will take place at God's appointed time. We know neither the day nor

the hour of His return, but we can be certain He will! Those who have received Christ as Lord and Savior will enjoy eternal bliss, those without Christ will suffer eternal damnation (Mt 24:36-37; Ac 1:11; Jn 5:28-29; 2 Pe 3:10; 1 Th 4:16, 18).

Why doesn't the C.D.H.A. have a set membership fee?

The Christian Deer Hunters Association® is a non-profit, interdenominational organization which has been incorporated in the state of Minnesota. The work of the association is financed solely through the gifts and contributions received from members and friends of the association.

It is our hope that all members will take seriously the responsibility that they have to help reach their fellow hunters for Jesus Christ. By not having a set membership fee, we are trusting all individuals to cheerfully honor their commitment to the Lord in accordance with their income (1 Corinthians 16:2; 2 Corinthians 9:7). Please be generous!

MEMBERSHIP BENEFITS

- C.D.H.A. Newsletter (published at least once annually).
- Complimentary copies of current C.D.H.A. literature.
- 1 C.D.H.A. cloth patch (initial membership only).
- An invitation to participate in various C.D.H.A. outreaches.
- 1 membership card.
- An awareness that you are helping to reach other hunters with the good news of Jesus Christ.
- The privilege of purchasing C.D.H.A. materials (as available) for personal use.

(No C.D.H.A. materials are to be sold for personal gain.)

Devotions for Deer Hunters

CHRISTIAN DEER HUNTERS ASSOCIATION® APPLICATION FOR ANNUAL MEMBERSHIP

Name:
Phone: (   )
Mailing Address:
City, State, Zip:

- I have been saved from the wrath of God by accepting Jesus Christ as my own personal Lord and Savior and am seeking to live by scriptural principles.
- I will support the work of God that the Christian Deer Hunters Association® is seeking to accomplish by means of my time, talents, and material treasures as the Lord allows.
- By the grace of God, I will adhere without reservation to the Christian Deer Hunters Association's Statement of Faith and will seek to support its purpose, goals, main objective, and resolutions. I understand that a failure to do so may result in my immediate removal from the membership in the C.D.H.A.

Signature:
Date:
Membership Renewal #:

Remove (or photocopy) and enclose with your donation. Make checks payable to Christian Deer Hunters Association® and mail to:

**Christian Deer Hunters Association®
PO Box 432
Silver Lake, MN 55381**

Amount Enclosed:

Sharing the Good News of Jesus Christ through:

National Booth Outreaches

Scriptures for the Stand

Trading Cards

Tracts

Postcards

Project Sponsor-A-Stand

World Wide Web

Evangelistic Materials for Game Feeds

. . . And Much More!

Order Form

____ *Devotions for Deer Hunters*: $14.95 U.S. (per copy).

____ $4.00 U.S. Shipping and handling for first copy for U.S. $2 Each additional copy. International orders add $3 for each copy.

Minnesota residents add 6.5% tax.

Bookstores and others interested in orders of ten books or more are eligible for the standard bookstore discount. For details contact the Christian Deer Hunters Association® at the address below.

1) Order online at http://www.christiandeerhunters.org
2) Mail this form with name, address, and payment to:
   Christian Deer Hunters Association®
   PO Box 432
   Silver Lake, MN 55381

Make check or money order payable to:
Christian Deer Hunters Association®

       TOTAL ENCLOSED_____